T0151508

Turning the Tide

Reawakening
the Woman's Heart and Soul

SUMA DIN

THE ISLAMIC
FOUNDATION

Turning the Tide: Reawakening the Woman's Heart and Soul

First published in England by
The Islamic Foundation
Markfield Conference Centre,
Ratby Lane Markfield,
Leicestershire LE67 9SY, United Kingdom
email: publications@islamic-foundation.com
Website: www.Islamic-foundation.com

Qur'an House, PO Box 30611, Nairobi, Kenya

PMB 3193, Kano, Nigeria

Distributed by
Kube Publishing Ltd.
Tel: +44(0)1530 249230
email: info@kubepublishing.com

Cataloguing-in-Publication Data is available from the British library

ISBN 978-0-86037-758-0 Hardback
ISBN 978-0-86037-729-0 ebook

Cover design and internal design: Jannah Haque
Typesetting: Nasir Cadir
Image Credits: Suma Din
Stock Photography: Fotolia
Printed by: Elma Basım, Turkey

In the Name of Allah, the Most Gracious, the Ever Merciful.

And He it is Who has created human beings from water:
then He established relationships of lineage and marriage:
for your Sustainer is ever infinite in His power.
(Surah *al-Furqān* 25:54)

And among His signs is this:
you see the earth barren and desolate.
Then when We send down water upon it,
it stirs and swells with life.
He Who brings it to life
can surely give life to the dead [of heart as well]
For indeed He has power over all things.
(Surah *Fuṣṣilāt* 41:39)

Endorsements

"A deeply poignant and meaningful book, that will take the soul on a journey of reflection and spiritual rejuvenation. The verses of the Qur'an and important life lessons that Suma Din opens our eyes to, will be as soul-quenching for today's generation as they were for the previous."
Sheikha Fatima Barkatulla

"*Turning the Tide* is written in a poetic and gentle way weaving in verses of the Qur'an and hadith alongside stories from the life of some of Islam's greatest female role models. Suma Din does a wonderful job inviting the reader to contemplate their faith in a deeper way through poetry, prose, and supplications."
A. Helwa,
Author of Bestselling title *Secrets of Divine Love*

"*Turning the Tide* is a lovely book that floats through the various seasons of a woman's life with gentleness and joy. Suma Din has collected verses, quotes, poems, and stories into categories that encourage the reader to think about her life stages. Whether you are thinking about birth or death, marriage or youthful energy you will find a lovely wave to ride in this lovely collection."

Dr. Tamara Gray,
Exec. Director & Chief Spirituality Officer, Rabata

"*Turning the Tide* is an inspirational, empowering book for Muslim Women. It gives an opportunity for the reader to reflect and find her voice. This is much needed in the current times, as many of the Muslim victims I support mistakenly think Islam supports their oppression, which is clearly wrong. It is a brilliant book."

Maryam Cairns,
Founder of Muslim Survivor of Domestic Violence,
Online Support for Muslim victims of abuse

"*Turning the Tide* is one of the most beautifully uplifting books for women of all ages and walks of life. In essence it speaks to the spiritual soul; bringing peace, solace, comfort and strength.

The sections on supplications are truly a nourishing balm for the soul and a source of contemplative comfort for those seeking a heartfelt connection with Allah. It includes a thought-provoking collection of reminders, poetry and soothing verses and quotes from the Qur'an and Sunnah. You will find yourself reaching out for this book in whatever difficulty or emotional turbulence you may be facing. It will serve as a spiritual guidebook to help one navigate through various stages of life."

Safura Houghton,
Muslim Chaplain, Founder of The Lantern Initiative

"*Turning the Tide* by Suma Din is a spiritually stirring, intellectually engaging and emotionally refreshing and gratifying work. For it awakens us out of our materialistic slumber to reflect on the numerous, life ennobling signs of Allah, to reorient us to our relationship with our Lord and Creator and to revitalize in us the meaning and purpose of life.

Symbolically and dexterously the story of a woman's life is interwoven with the account of water, the source of life. The creative and comforting roles of both are enunciated as Allah's bounties which we should acknowledge with utmost gratitude. This exquisite work serves as dhikr (remembrance of Allah), hamd (praise of Allah) and tasbih (glorification of Allah)."

Professor Abdur Raheem Kidwai,
Aligarh Muslim University, Author of the *Daily Wisdom Series*

"16 years ago, I was blessed with the gift of coming across *Turning the Tide*. I was a new Muslim of 5 years and had given birth to my first child. Reading through this deep ocean of spiritual literary brilliance, I found beauty, comfort and most importantly an invitation to a renewed relationship between my soul and her Lord. My soul had embarked upon a journey in choosing Islam. My body had endured a physical journey in becoming a mother. *Turning the Tide* was then, and still very much is today, a soothing balm, a celebration of womanhood and a special invitation to worship Allah with excellence.

The call to spirituality flows throughout the book as elegantly as the author has used the metaphor of water. This, coupled with the way the author sanctifies each stage of a woman's life, makes it relatable and applicable to all - regardless of age, race or life's circumstances.

The myriad of voices in each section is gentle, vulnerable and authentic. Through these poetic reflections, the female reader feels understood; her circumstances mirrored through words that depict an honest experience of being a believer and a woman. *Turning the Tide* doesn't stop there. The authentic experience of the believing woman is honoured and the author then compassionately encourages us to aim for The Most High, Allah, through dua, words from our Lord and advice from His Messenger (saw).

We are provided with a celebration of our unique experience and at the same time we are encouraged to become better, stronger and most importantly closer to Allah. This makes *Turning the Tide* the deep ocean of spiritual beauty that it is.

Reading it 16 years later, there's so much more I've taken from it. I'm older, my children are older. I'm no longer a new Muslim. But I'm still a believing woman. Alhamdulillah. It's a book to read at the different stages of your life. I invite all to dive in and be ready to be delighted."

Aliyah Quadri (Umm Raiyaan)
Founder and CEO of Solace UK,
Co-Host of Honest Tea Talk

"I read the first edition of *Turning the Tide* many years ago. The myriad of voices spoke to me then, as a young woman searching for her own voice, and they speak to me now, the voices of so many women, in harmony with my voice. Suma has beautifully interwoven her own deeply soulful voice in this text; words that

flow from heart to heart, reawakening the myriad of voices in the reader. A stirring read, a spiritual journey."
Waheeda Islam,
Psychotherapist and Operations Coordinator for Nour Domestic Violence Charity

"In Suma's *Turning the Tide* she combines a unique way of a woman's journey with her poetic flair. If you're looking for a book that allows you to feel - then this is for you. I hope every woman is able to resonate with this through its apt hadiths, Qur'anic verses, poems, and personal touch. The concept of the book was nothing like I've read before and I was left feeling inspired by Suma who ultimately realigned our purpose within the book, allowing us to see our journey through a new lens."
inspirited Minds, www.inspiritedminds.org.uk

Contents

Acknowledgements

There are several people to thank for the book you hold in your hands. First and foremost, is my gratitude to Allah *subḥānahu wa taʿālā,* Our Creator and Sustainer for granting me the opportunity to take an idea through to completion. All praise belongs to Allah *subḥānahu wa taʿālā* for whatever good is derived from this and I seek His forgiveness for any mistakes and shortcomings.

I started jotting ideas down on paper for this book in 2000, as a full time mum of two very young girls and expecting our third baby. I therefore owe huge thanks to many people around that time that quietly supported the notion of this book, as that is all it was for a while, until the first edition that came out in 2004. The completion of this book would never have happened were it not for the encouragement of Abdul Wahid Hamid (author of *Islam the Natural Way* and *Companions of the Prophet*) and his generosity in sharing his knowledge of Qur'anic Arabic to guide the selections. At the same time, he answered my numerous questions and allayed my doubts and worries about whether this book should exist in the first place. I will always be indebted to him for his support.

Heartfelt thanks to many friends for reading drafts of the first manuscript and making valuable suggestions. As the years have rolled on and brought us to this fourth edition, I am grateful for our conversations and debates, for our mental gymnastics as we have grown together over the years. Thank you for your thoughts and feedback on snippets that I added to this version – you know who you are! Sometimes complete strangers have had an impact on the contents of this book and I thank them too for the valuable conversations we've had that taught me a great deal. Although I've never encountered them again, their presence lingers in this book like the fragrance of honeysuckle in the evening.

Much appreciation is due to the publishers. I'm very grateful for the manuscript receiving the attention and guidance of Professor Kidwai and Dr. Manazir Ahsan, along with their publication staff at the Islamic Foundation who prepared the first edition all those years ago. Subsequently, I thank editors of previous editions, the present Director, Haris Ahmad, the designer Jannah Haque and the staff at Kube Publishing who have supported *Turning the Tide* through significant revisions to this fourth edition.

A family's relationship to book writing is a precarious one; supportive and encouraging on the one hand, whilst enduring the whole messy business of writing, on the other. And my family has walked through this all. I'm grateful to my, now adult children for exploring some of the themes in this edition with enthusiasm and raw honesty that comes with their youth. The many extended family members are also thanked for voicing their interest and discussing themes; whether close to home or on other sides of the globe, thank you all!

Whilst I know he would prefer not to be acknowledged in writing, I am always grateful to my husband, Asad, for his support, sage advice and unwavering vision to keep our sights on the only destination that matters.

Above everyone, parents make the biggest sacrifices and investment in their children even if they are not directly involved in a book's production! I remain totally indebted and thankful to my mother and father for all that they have done and pray that any good that comes from this work benefits them too. May Allah *subḥānahu wa taʿālā* grant His mercy and a place in Jannah for my father who has departed from this world. Ameen.

Introduction

Every era in the history of the world has presented different challenges to a woman's growth: challenges to the woman's right to be educated, challenges to her equitable treatment with male siblings, challenges indeed to her very existence. Many of the past wrongs have been corrected only to be replaced by newer insidious ones, yet still there is a collective feeling of searching, questioning and evaluating one's own self worth as a woman.

On the face of things, opportunities abound for women, empowering them to fulfil their ambitions and use their abilities. Nonetheless, the need to delve deeper and understand more about our identities refuses to go away. The soul of each woman is not fulfilled with material prosperity alone, or better prospects in terms of social relationships. There persists a need for inner harmony and a life of balance in which the deep yearnings of the soul can be satisfied.

Turning the Tide is about turning away from the restrictive beliefs, habits and fads that have starved women spiritually. It is about turning towards the eternal message of the Qur'an and Prophetic wisdom, the primary sources of Islam. Where better to find the contentedness and wholeness each being seeks than from the Creator of each being. He Who knows our strengths and our weaknesses and our most intimate needs.

This book takes a chronological journey through the stages of a woman's life and looks at the value and inherent worth of each stage. Within the world and cosmos around us lie a host of natural signs (*āyāts*) to consider and reflect upon. There are stages and cycles in natural phenomena everywhere – from the faraway planets down to the core of this earth. Every aspect of our environment is designed by the Creator for us to benefit or learn from. It is in this vein that the imagery of water flows through the book as an extended metaphor, reflecting facets of our selves as well as reminding us of God's miracles surrounding us.

Water is the source of all life on earth. Women and water share a close relationship; after all, a mother-to-be carries life in the first home of water. Water for our health, in our daily lives and even the teardrops that well up in our eyes, are all a mercy from God. Water is also a great calming and healing fluid. A Muslim's life is inextricably tied to purifying oneself by washing with water before offering prayers through the day. Water thus becomes part of worship, part of living, part of being revitalised.

Unity in the world, unity in its creation, unity in our creation, are the simple precepts upon which stands the universal truth of Islam. The understanding of the Qur'an is inextricably tied to the manifestations of the Creator's signs on earth.

I hope that together, the Qur'anic verses, *aḥādīth*, and glimpses of our surroundings will bring a fresh perspective to our lives through the passage of time. May they energise the reader to use her esteemed role with confidence and humility.

Dedication

Dear Reader,

When you journey with Turning the Tide, *you'll find a space of comfort, hope and affirmation, of homecoming. You can set aside the tools you toil and labour with in your daily lives and enter this replenishing ocean.*

Deep beneath the surface of the ocean lies its soul; the sea life, flora and fauna, igniting coral – an endangered world. Deep beneath the surface of another body – our physical frame – lies our soul; the delicate and enduring, the unseen as it teems with eternal life – an endangered world. Beneath the body of both waters, what lays hidden is prone to being forgotten.

This edition of Turning the Tide *emphasises the inner, the struggles, the hairline fractures in our soul that no one other than Allah subḥānahu wa taʿālā knows about. In the time between the first edition and this, the fourth one, the world has moved in unanticipated new directions. The exterior, the momentary 'image' of people's lives has become a new form of existing, which many subscribe to without question. In contrast, daily, real life is what it always has been: a delicate shift of tones, unflattering and murky on one day, transparent and lucid on another. The changes made in this edition peel away at surface layers to uncover raw honesty. This edition adjusts the mast of this ship we call life, to sail towards the simplicity of the āyāts (signs) around us and find inspiration in what is easily overlooked; the shoreline, those drops of rain, the clouds.*

Any good that comes from this book is from Allah subḥānahu wa taʿālā, and any mistakes are mine and I seek al-Ghaffār's forgiveness for those. Ultimately, I seek His acceptance for the intention behind this work; this, and this alone is all that really matters.

Your sister,
Suma

Dedication

A Map for Your Journey

Each of the chapters in *Turning the Tide* has the same layered format. Below is a map of these layers.

- *Introduction* and *Myriad Voices* ~ Each chapter begins with a brief introduction to the stage of life it covers, followed by 'Myriad Voices' which are fictional voices that are placed like parts of a mosaic to create pictures of our emotions. I wrote these to reflect some aspects of a woman's thoughts; her questions and contemplations, her anxieties and hopes. As the mural of life is far greater than what these voices portray, adding your own inner expression to each chapter will enrich your reading. Once this background is explored the rest of each chapter consists of:

- *Translations of verses from the Qur'an and Aḥādīth* ~ The translated verses comprise the body of the text, giving the Islamic perspective on various issues raised through the chapter. The Qur'an is God's words in the Arabic language.

There is one Qur'an that exists in the world; there are no other versions or adaptations. Any translation is not the Qur'an, but an *explanation* of its meaning – often requiring a variety of words and phrases to explain one Arabic word in the text. The order of words and grammar in the Qur'an, however, have never changed and remain – as promised by the Almighty – preserved exactly as they were revealed to the Prophet Muhammad, peace and blessings of God be upon him, by the angel Jibrīl.

- *Hadith* ~ A hadith is a saying of the Prophet Muhammad, peace and blessings of God be upon him, which marks his approval and consent of an action, or explanation of a verse from the Qur'an. The hadith quoted are from the works of the major compilers: Muslim, Bukhārī, Abū Dāwūd, Ibn Mājah, Aḥmad, Tirmdhī and Nisā'ī.

- *Du'ā's* ~ These are supplications which address God Almighty directly. Many supplications exist in the Qur'an and the Prophet, peace be upon him, taught many *du'ā's* to help people for a whole host of needs and concerns. Supplications can of course be made in one's own words.

- *Noble Women* ~ This final layer is a glimpse of the life of a righteous woman who exemplifies qualities related to the chapter. Some are portrayed in the Qur'an as examples to humanity, others are blessed women related to the Prophet, upon whom be peace, who were assured of their place in Paradise.

A Note on the Language

While I hope this book will inspire many beyond the binary
of Muslim and non-Muslim, I have used language throughout
which addresses a believer – one who accepts the Qur'an as the
final revelation of God and Muhammad, peace and blessings
of God be upon him, as the last messenger in the line of
Prophets, starting from Adam to Noah, to Moses, Abraham
and all those in between.

Allah is the Arabic for The One True God, Creator and
Sustainer of the Universe. Both the Arabic and the English
have been used in the text.

- ﷺ This is the Arabic for 'peace and blessings be upon him',
  following the name of Prophet Muhammad ﷺ.

- ؓ / ؓ means '*raḍiyallāhu anhu / hā*', 'May Allah be pleased
  with him/her'.

'My rights are sent from above. They are from *al-Karīm*,
the Most Gracious. I have been given a rightful place on
God's earth to grow into the role of one who invites to good.
For this, I need my heart to be educated and nourished.'

'Who will speak for me?
I had a life, as valid as yours, as "alive" as you are now.
I breathed, moved, sensed, understood and was learning about
my world.
I could not speak
Who will speak for me?
I could not say I wanted to live.
I had no voice to ask what crime I had committed.
My life was taken before I entered the world.
My heartbeat was my only voice.
It screamed:
"Alive, alive, alive."
But they wouldn't listen.
Who will speak for me?'

The Soul
Wide Oceans

And it is He Who has brought you into being from a single entity.
(Surah *al-An'ām* 6:99)

Consider the human soul and the One Who shaped and gave it balance, how He imbued it with its capacity for moral failing as well as its God-consciousness.
(Surah *al-Shams* 91:7–8)

The Soul

The soul is that part of us that is an intangible reality, permanent yet elusive, constantly present yet unseen. Our soul is our centre, and the essence of our being.

To know ourselves, we need to recognise our souls. Before our time on earth began, our souls agreed to submit to *al-Khāliq* – the Creator who determines the nature and constitution of every creation. The One God, Allah.

Your soul in its original, pure state made this covenant. It agreed to worship none other than the One God. Now, in the soul's earthly stay, it has an innate draw towards God and His wondrous signs. Every soul searches for inner peace, to be in harmony with its nature; it was designed this way. In today's world, with its fixation on meeting physical and material desires alone, the soul is starved and seeks refuge in a variety of ways to 'forget' its emptiness. Still, the longing remains – the longing for a connection to the One greater than our selves.

You were entrusted with your soul, and the covenant it made. In your care, the soul needs to be nurtured on the remembrance of God. It needs to be fed on the contemplation of His innumerable signs in the vast cosmos and within the human self. It needs to be sustained by the grace of God and by seeking His guidance and forgiveness.

As water is the source of life on earth, our soul is the core of our being. It is unique and subtle like the ineffable clearness of water. It is free from anyone's grasp. When our souls are valued and strengthened, then will we find our capacity and our worth, as deep and expansive as the widest ocean. Our soul, like the ocean, has a delicate balance where it's 'health' is vital to humanity's survival. A thriving ocean's chemistry is best measured by its unseen floor, where it absorbs everything around it. How similar to the health of our invisible souls, in need of protection and investment if they are to be the life force they were created to be.

Myriad Voices

'Where was my soul?
In the space between consciousness and the unconsciousness, where
was my soul?
Through the rhythm of sleeping and waking, where is my soul?
As I drift in this earthly body, sleeping, waking, sleeping, waking,
sleeping, waking,
sleeping, weeping. Seeking… where is my soul?'

'Once, long ago, the soul was nurtured on the remembrance of its
Creator. It was moulded and shaped, guided towards truth and
balance-checking desires. Therefore, the soul found peace and,
desiring good in all things, reached great heights.

What's happened to the soul today? This is an age when carnal
desires and "instant" pleasure and satisfaction have become the
purpose of living. Every precious sense of the human being –
taste, touch, sound, smell and sight – is gratified. No detail or
comfort is overlooked.

The needs of the soul are neglected.
Spiritual needs go unnoticed.
Left aside, an outdated accessory.

The soul today is left to collapse and descend into annihilation,
taking with it the heart and mind in a downward spiral, into
the abyss of despair and conflict.'

'I, your Soul, am the core of your being, the subtle reality.
I am Divinely created, and enter this world pure.
Before your bones and flesh took shape, I was there.
Present in the darkness of eternity, in the space between life
and death.
Before your voice echoed your thoughts,
I spoke in unison with all humanity and affirmed Him
as My Sustainer,
Creator of the Heavens and the earth.
Before your ears, the channel to your heart heard the sounds
of this world,
I heard His call to worship and believe.'

'Until my spiritual needs to know
and remember God are satisfied,
I shall not be at peace.'

'Look inside for contentment.
In stillness, silence, solitude,
we can hear the whisper of contentment,
Like the whirling
in the seashell held up to our ears:
It was always there,
inside us,
not out
by the
sea...'

The Eternal Sources

The *nafs* (self) and *rūḥ* (soul) was brought into being by God, *al-Bāriʿ* – the Creator – who brings into existence a being out of nothing. The soul is entrusted to its owner to be cared for until it journeys back to God.

God is the Creator of all things, and He is the Guardian and Disposer of all affairs. (Surah *al-Zumar* 39:62)

He is God, the Creator, the Maker, the Bestower of forms and appearances. To Him belong all the most beautiful attributes of perfection. Whatever is in the heavens and on earth declares His Praises and Glory: and He is the Exalted in Might, the Wise. (Surah *al-Ḥashr* 59:24)

And We have created the human being in the best of moulds. (Surah *al-Tīn* 95:4)

It is Allah who begins the creation then repeats it. Then shall you all be brought back to Him. (Surah *al-Rūm*, 30:11)

'Your Sustainer has a right over you, your soul has a right over you, and your family has a right over you; so you should fulfil the rights of all those who have rights over you.' The advice of Salmān al-Fārisī, a Companion of the Prophet 🪷, to Abū Darda. (Bukhārī)

'Everyone starts his day and is a vendor of his soul, either freeing it or bringing about its ruin.' (Muslim)

The soul lives beyond the boundaries of earthly existence into the Hereafter. This is central to our destiny.

And they ask you [O Muhammad] about the rūḥ. Say: 'The knowledge of the rūḥ *is with my Sustainer. Of its knowledge you have been given only a little.'* (Surah *Banī Isrā īl* 17:85)

God is He Who excelled in the creation of everything that He has created. He began the creation of the human being from clay, then He made his progeny from an extraction of a mean fluid [from the male and female].

Then He fashioned him in due proportion and breathed into him something of His spirit, and He gave you the faculties of hearing, sight, feeling and understanding. And yet, little are the thanks you give! (Surah *al-Sajdah* 32:7–9)

The soul, the heart and the mind were all created in balance, in the state of fiṭrah – the natural state of the human being. When the souls were created, they agreed to the covenant, accepting Allah as their Lord, and it is this that opens up inner eyes to recognising the truth.

Allah has endeared faith [īmān] to you and made it beautiful in your hearts. (Surah *al-Ḥujurāt* 49:7)

Our Sustainer is He Who gave to each [created] thing its form and nature, and further, gave [it] guidance. (Surah *Ṭā' Hā'* 20:50)

On no soul do We place a burden greater than it can bear. Before Us is a record which clearly shows the truth. They will never be wronged. (Surah *al-Mu'minūn* 23:62)

No misfortune can happen on earth or in your souls but is recorded in a decree before We bring it into existence. That is truly easy for God. (Surah *al-Ḥadīd* 57:22)

'Virtue is that which your soul and heart feel satisfied with. Sin is that which troubles the soul and about which the heart is uneasy and confused, even though people may give their legal opinions in its favour.' (Muslim)

'He is successful whose heart Allah has made sincere towards faith, whose heart He has made free from unbelief, his tongue truthful, his soul calm, his nature straight, whose ear He has made attentive and his eye observant. The ear is a funnel and the eye is a repository for what the heart learns. Successful is the one whose heart is made retentive.' (Aḥmad)

Nourishing our souls requires coming closer to Allah through His remembrance, contemplating His signs all around us, seeking knowledge and following a virtuous way of life.

Remain then conscious of God as best you can, and listen [to Him] and pay heed. And spend in charity for the good of your own selves: for such as are saved from their own covetousness, it is they who shall prosper. (Surah *al-Taghābun* 64:16)

And be steadfast in Prayer, and regular in charity. And whatever good you send forth for your souls before you, you shall find it with Allah, for Allah sees all that you do. (Surah *al-Baqarah* 2:110)

Say: 'Shall I seek for my cherisher other than God, when He is the Cherisher of all things that exist?' Every soul draws the mead of its acts on none but itself. No bearer of burdens can bear the burdens of another. Your goal in the end is towards God, and He will then tell you the truth of the things wherein you disputed. (Surah *al-An'ām* 6:164)

And keep your soul content with those who call on their Sustainer morning and evening, seeking His countenance; and let not your eyes pass beyond them, seeking the pomp and glitter of this life; nor obey any whose heart We have permitted to neglect the remembrance of Us, one who follows his own desires, whose case has gone beyond all bounds. (Surah *al-Kahf* 18:28)

And the likeness of those who spend their substance, seeking to please Allah and to strengthen their souls, is as a garden, high and fertile. Heavy rain falls on it and makes it yield a double increase of harvest. And if it receives not heavy rain, a light drizzle will suffice. Allah sees well whatever you do. (Surah *al-Baqarah* 2:265)

Every soul will be held in pledge for its deeds. (Surah *Muddaththir* 74:38)

The achievement for the balanced, conscious soul is, through the grace of God, contentment in this life and eternal peace. We are promised justice, as God is *al-'Adl*, the Just, for the soul that is consistently God-conscious.

Whoever submits his whole self to Allah and is a doer of good will get his reward with his Sustainer. On such shall be no fear, nor shall they grieve. (Surah *al-Baqarah,* 2:112)

Those who spend [on others], whether in prosperity or in adversity; who restrain anger, and pardon [all] people. Allah loves those who do good.

And those who, having done something to be ashamed of, or wronged their own souls, earnestly bring Allah to mind, and ask for forgiveness for their sins – and who can forgive sins except Allah? – and do not knowingly persist in [the wrong] they have done.

For such the reward is forgiveness from their Sustainer, and Gardens through which rivers flow – an eternal dwelling: How excellent a reward for those who work [and strive]. (Surah *Āl 'Imrān* 3:134–136)

It will be no more than a single Blast, and lo they will all be brought before Us. Then, on that Day, not a soul will be wronged in the least, and you shall all but be repaid for your past Deeds. Indeed, the Companions of the Garden shall that day have joy in all that they do.

They and their associates will be in groves of [cool] shade, reclining on couches with all kinds of fruit to eat, and they shall have whatever they call for.

'Peace!' shall be the word [of salutation] from an Ever Merciful Sustainer. (Surah *Yā Sīn* 36:53–58)

[To the righteous soul, it will be said]: 'O you satisfied soul!
Return to your Sustainer, well pleased, and well pleasing
unto Him!
Enter, then, among My servants! Enter My Paradise!'
(Surah *al-Fajr* 89:27–30)

Du'ā' – Supplications

'*Du'ā'* is the essence of worship.'
(Tirmidhī)

Allah is *al-Samī'*, the Hearer of prayer.

Within each of us lies a space that is only filled when we communicate with God. *Du'ā's*, or supplications, are that channel for addressing God, without any intermediary. They are the expression of hope, knowing that God ultimately writes our destinies and is the Ever Merciful. Supplications rest on complete trust in God for relief and ease, for forgiveness and fulfilling our needs. They are the balm for the soul, in unending supply. A person may not realize they are in prayer, but when their hearts call out for help, for relief from *al-Laṭīf,* the Subtle, for tranquillity that no person or object can give – this is 'making *du'ā'.*

Although they are a personal expression, the Prophet's *du'ā's,* just like those of earlier Prophets, were infused by a sense of social responsibility. He constantly prayed for the best for humankind, for those who believe, for those near us and those far from us in time and distance. Hence, many *du'ā's* begin with 'we' and 'us'. The focus of many supplications is the love for humanity, to which we all belong.

Supplications can be made in one's own language. The open hearts and the desire to seek God's pleasure, to seek the good in this life and the Hereafter, is where the communication starts – whatever one's language. Along with this, there are many *du'ā's* from the Qur'an and what the noble Messenger of God – Muhammad ﷺ taught his Companions and family.

The Prophet ﷺ was once asked, 'What supplication finds the greatest acceptance?' He replied, 'A prayer offered in the middle of the latter part of the night and after the prescribed Prayers.' The last third of the night is a time of stillness which is ideal for contemplation and drawing closer to God. It has been said by the Prophet ﷺ 'God is the nearest to His servant in midst of the later part of the night and if you are able to be amongst those who remember God at that hour, do so.' (Tirmidhī)

There are many blessed times when believers are encouraged to turn their attention towards their inner needs by making *du'ā'*. Amongst the various times that are blessed, is the month of Ramadan, the time of the pilgrimage – hajj, every Friday, when a person is travelling and when one is ill. On a daily basis, the prostrations during the prescribed five prayers are opportune times. The Prophet of God ﷺ also stated that the supplications of three people are not refused: a fasting person when breaking the fast, a just ruler, and an oppressed person. (Tirmidhī)

'The Messenger of Allah ﷺ said: "The closest the servant can be to Allah is when he is prostrating to Him, so increase your supplications then."' (Muslim)

One can become disheartened sometimes, with a feeling that their prayers are not answered. The Prophet ﷺ said, 'No one makes a *du'ā'* without God giving him what he asks for, or keeping away from him a similar amount of evil, provided he does not ask for something sinful or the breaking of family ties.' (Tirmidhī) Also, 'Ā'ishah ﷺ is reported to have said, 'No believer makes *du'ā'* and it is wasted. Either it is granted here in this world or deposited for him in the Hereafter as long as he does not get frustrated.'

'Nothing prevents what has been decreed except supplication to God.'

Lā yaraḍu al-qaḍā' illā al-du'ā'.

(Saying of Prophet Muhammad ﷺ; Tirmidhī)

Tell them, [O Prophet]: 'O my people who have transgressed against yourselves, do not despair of God's Mercy; surely God forgives sins altogether; surely He is the All Forgiving, the Most Compassionate'. (Surah *al-Zumar* 39:53)

Du'ā's for Our Soul

[We indeed heard a crier, saying]: 'Our Sustainer! Forgive us our sins, blot out from us our iniquities and take to Thyself our souls in the company of the righteous'. (Surah *Āl 'Imrān* 3:193)

'O Allah, I seek refuge in You from incapacity and sloth, from cowardice and miserliness, from drowning in debt and the overpowering of men.

'O Allah, grant to my soul its sense of righteousness and purify it, for You are the Best Purifier thereof. You are its Protecting friend and its Guardian.

'O Allah, I seek refuge in You from knowledge which does not benefit, from a heart that does not fear (You), from a soul that is not content and from a supplication that is not answered.' (Muslim)

'O my Sustainer! In Your Name I lay my side on this bed and in Your Name I will lift it up therefrom. If You take my soul, bestow mercy on it, and if You release it, protect it as You protect Your righteous servants.' (Bukhārī)

'O Allah, I have indeed oppressed my soul excessively and none can forgive sins except You. So forgive me with forgiveness from Yourself and have mercy upon me. Surely, You are the most Forgiving, the ever Merciful.' (Bukhārī)

Trusting in Her Sustainer, Unrelenting in Belief

The Lady Hajirah ﷺ
Mother of the Prophet Ismā ʿīl ﷺ and Wife of the Prophet Ibrāhīm ﷺ

In every direction she looked there was no sign of life. Just mountains. Their rugged, steep sides were the only features that interrupted the miles of desert all around her. Isolated and desolate was the bleak valley of Makkah. The sky was indeed her canopy, the sand beneath her feet her home.

Yet her husband, the Divinely-guided Prophet Ibrāhīm ﷺ had brought her here, obeying the command to leave his wife and child in this wilderness. And he prayed:

> *Our Sustainer! Indeed I have settled some*
> *of my offspring*
> *to dwell in a valley without cultivation,*
> *by Thy Sacred House;*
> *in order, O our Sustainer, that they may*
> *establish regular Prayer:*
> *so fill the hearts of some among men*
> *with love towards them,*
> *and feed them with fruits: so that they may give*
> *thanks.* (Surah *Ibrāhīm* 14:37)

Having travelled the long distance from Palestine to this valley in the Ḥijāz together, the time had now come for Ibrāhīm ﷺ, who loved his wife and son dearly, to part from them. As he

turned to make the long journey back, his wife Hajirah ☙
asked him:

'Did Allah tell you to do this (were you inspired by God to do
this)?' 'Yes,' he replied.
'Then He will not forsake us and He will not let us perish,'
responded Hajirah ☙.

Hajirah's soul was strong with faith in her Creator and
Sustainer. She accepted the test placed upon herself and her
family. Her unshakable trust in God gave her hope in the face
of any person's worst fear: total isolation.

What little dates and water she had for herself and her young
baby were soon finished, whilst the thirsty cries of the infant
rose in urgency. Each way Hajirah ☙ looked she could not
see any water. Unable to feed her child, the maternal force
at the core of each mother spurred her to run to a nearby
mound. She climbed it some way, desperate to gain sight of
something – anything – to save her child. Seeing nothing she
turned to another mound some distance away, ascending that
one too and searching earnestly. Seven times, the noble lady
Hajirah ☙ ran between the two hillocks. Then she returned
to where the baby Ismāʿīl lay and cried out for help from her
Sustainer. Her prayer was answered, and when she looked
down she saw water miraculously gushing forth from where
her son's heels had struck the sand as he cried. As the water
welled up from the ground, Hajirah ☙ hastened to build up a
wall of mud around it to arrest it from flowing away. This was
the origin of the ancient well of Zamzam.

The mother quenched her thirst then fed her child. But this was far more than just water coming forth from the arid land. This was the beginning of life, of a prosperous town; the centre of monotheism for all time to come. Soon after this valley was blessed with water birds flocked to the place to drink, and the flight of the birds led caravans of traders to the same valley. The continuous flow of the pure life-sustaining water encouraged them to settle there – with Hajirah's permission – and it was not long before the valley was inhabited. The fortitude of one female soul prepared the ground for the historic building of the Kaaba which Ibrāhīm 🕮 returned to build with his son, Ismāʿīl 🕮, by the will of God.

Today, the two mounds the lady Hajirah 🕮 ran between are called Safa and Marwah. From the time the pilgrimage to Makkah – the hajj – was Divinely ordained on believers until the present day, every person male and female traces the steps of this strong woman – Hajirah 🕮 – the wife of one Prophet and mother to another. Her unshakeable spirit is commemorated as an essential rite of pilgrimage and serves as a reminder to all on their spiritual journey. Both her courage and wisdom are embedded in the sacred land of Makkah.

Hajirah's call to the Almighty God was for sustenance in a barren valley. Her prayer was answered. May our own calls to God from the landscape of barren hearts meet with such a bounteous response.

Childhood
Snowflake
Crystals

*God creates you in the wombs of your mothers, one act
of creation after another, in three veils of darkness.*
(**Surah** *al-Zumar* 39:6)

Childhood

Childhood is innocence. The newborn enters this world dependent on those around them for love and protection. Each being arrives here free of any sin, unblemished by anyone else's past deeds.

Regardless of our age, childhood is the one phase of life that we are all bound to. You may not have children in your life at all, but you are the child of your parents. Your childhood is a part of you that shaped who you are today. The ties remain strong, however far in time and distance you may travel from those innocent years. A rhyme, a fragrance, a particular taste from the past, evokes strong childhood memories. These are the years when the foundation stones were laid upon which lives are built.

If you have been blessed with the gift of children, they are a trust to you – an *amānah*. They are in your care for an appointed time to receive the individual nurturing, love and guidance that is rightly theirs.

Our natural surroundings distil aspects of our own selves. When snow falls it brings with it peace and serenity. Snowflakes appear all the same, being part of the larger white landscape, yet each single flake is a crystal, intricately proportioned. Delicate, with its own exceptional pattern, the form and star-like shapes are astounding.

So too is each and every child precious in his or her own pattern. Just as no two snowflake crystals share the same structure, so are no two children identical in thoughts, actions and aspirations. This individuality is imprinted on our fingertips, reinforcing our uniqueness. The unique crystals of snowflakes are shaped according to the temperatures they pass through when falling from the clouds. Similarly, children are affected by the atmosphere around them; in this lies their innocence and in this lies the responsibility to fulfil every child's right to a safe and loving environment to thrive, wherever they are on this earth.

Myriad Voices

'Giver of Life, my birth, by Your will
Brings gratefulness and joy.
My new, innocent being enters the world,
Wrapped in mercy and love.
"*Allāhu Akbar, Allāhu Akbar* – God is Most Great,
God is Most Great."
Primal words in my ears plant the roots of my being.
Deep grow these roots as I reach towards the light.'

'I am a trust, an *amānah*, not a possession. Born in total
innocence, I am close to my Creator. I trust in Him totally,
and thus I am free of all worry and anxiety. I have yet to learn
of these states.'

'I need care, protection and love. I need to be taught, but
also have much to teach those around me. I am spontaneous,
honest, very forgiving and look for the good in all around me.
When it rains, I see rainbows in droplets, and not the grey
clouds. My relationships are simple and without pretence.
I am uneducated in the artistry of human relationships.'

'I, your
Childhood,
am a
part of you.
The spine to
which all the
pages in your
book,
all the chapters
of your life
will be bound
and joined to.'

'My mother always said girls bring peace to a home. The day had come when the gift of peace was arriving, and the doors of our heart were open wide to welcome her in. So many years had elapsed and the desire for a child had not waned nor weakened. To raise another human, whom God had chosen to live on this earth, whose heart, mind and soul we were to warm and cherish, was a dream that always seemed remote. The day she arrived, our dreams finally took a real and tangible shape. As we looked into her bewildered, searching eyes we saw not our reflections, but a reminder of true innocence and helplessness. Allah had blessed us with so much to give. Now there was someone, orphaned from birth, with so much to receive.'

'My rights are sent from above. They are from *al-Karīm*,
the Most Gracious. I have been given a rightful place on
God's earth to grow into the role of one who invites to good.
For this, I need my heart to be educated and nourished.'

'Who will speak for me?
I had a life, as valid as yours, as "alive" as you are now.
I breathed, moved, sensed, understood and was learning about
my world.
I could not speak
Who will speak for me?
I could not say I wanted to live.
I had no voice to ask what crime I had committed.
My life was taken before I entered the world.
My heartbeat was my only voice.
It screamed:
"Alive, alive, alive."
But they wouldn't listen.
Who will speak for me?'

The Eternal Sources

When *al-Barr* – the Source of Goodness – decrees, a new being enters this world; a miracle beyond what any hand or mind can create. Each new-born girl and boy is valuable, neither superior to the other and equally deserving of care and protection. The arrival of this individual, pure and free of sin, is an occasion for gratitude and celebration.

We have created you then formed you. (Surah *al-Aʿrāf* 7:11)

He is God, the Creator, the Maker, the Bestower of forms.
To Him belong the most beautiful attributes of perfection.
(Surah *al-Ḥashr* 59:24)

It is He Who has created you all from dust, then from a sperm-drop, then from a leech-like clot; then does He get you out [into the light] as a child: then lets you [grow and] reach your age of full strength; then lets you become old, though of you there are some who die before; and lets you reach a term appointed, in order that you may learn wisdom. (Surah *al-Muʾmin* 40:67)

It is He who fashioned you in the wombs as He pleases. There is none worthy of worship except Him, the Almighty, the All Wise. (Surah *Āl ʿImrān* 3:6)

It is He Who brought you all forth from the wombs of your mothers when you knew nothing; and He gave you hearing and sight and intelligence and affections – that you may give thanks [to Him]. (Surah *al-Naḥl* 16:78)

And He has given you shape, and made your shapes beautiful and has provided for your sustenance. (Surah *al-Mu'min* 40:64)

To God belongs the dominion of the heavens and the earth. He creates what He wills [and plans]. He bestows [children] male or female according to His will [and plan]. (Surah *al-Shūrā* 42:49)

His command, when He intends a thing, is that He says to it, 'Be!' – and it is. (Surah *Yā Sīn* 36:82)

Children enter a world in which the needs of their body, mind and soul must be met. They have the right to justice and equity, kindness and guidance. Each child has the innate need to know its Creator.

Kill not your children out of the fear of poverty. We shall provide sustenance for them as well as for you. The killing of them is certainly an enormous sin. (Surah *Banī Isrā'īl* 17:31)

'The Prophet of God ﷺ said: "He is not one of us who has no affection for the young and no respect for the old, and who does not enjoin good and forbid wrong."' (Aḥmad)

'A father gives a child nothing better than a good education.' (Tirmidhī)

'The one who brings up two girls properly until they grow up, he and I would come (close together like this) on the Day of Resurrection' (and he interlaced his fingers). (Muslim)

'Jabir ibn Abdullah ﷺ reported that the Prophet ﷺ said:

"Whoever has three daughters and he accommodates them, shows mercy towards them, and supports them, Paradise is definitely guaranteed for him". Someone asked the Prophet ﷺ, "what if they are two daughters only?" He replied, "(He gets that reward,) even if they are (only) two."
Be generous to your children and excel in teaching them the best of conduct.' (Ibn Mājah)

'Don't pray against yourselves, nor your children, nor your belongings. There is the possibility that your prayer may synchronize with the time when Allah is about to confer upon you what you ask and thus your prayer may be readily answered.' (Abū Dāwūd)

'Fear Allah, and be just to your children.' (Bukhārī)

As years pass, the tapestry of relationships grows. Distinct threads are all woven together for one ultimate purpose: to submit to Allah, *al-Ḥayy*, the Living; *al-Mālik*, the Master and Owner of all that exists.

O humankind! Be conscious of your Sustainer, and fear [the coming of] a Day when no father can be of any benefit to his son, nor can a son be of any benefit to his father. The promise of God is certainly true. Let not then this present life deceive you, nor let the chief deceiver deceive you about God. (Surah *Luqmān* 31:33)

Know that this world's life is only sport and play and outward splendour and boasting among yourselves, and a vying in the multiplication of wealth and children. [It is] like the rain, whose causing the vegetation to grow pleases the tillers of the soil. Then the vegetation withers away and you will see it become yellow; then it becomes dried up and broken down. And in the Hereafter is a severe chastisement and [also] forgiveness from Allah and [His] pleasure; and this world's life is nothing but a means of deception. (Surah *al-Ḥadīd* 57:20)

And know that your possessions and your children are a test, and that with Allah is a mighty reward. (Surah *al-Anfāl* 8:28)

O you who believe! Let not your riches or your children divert you from the remembrance of Allah. If any act thus, the loss is their own. (Surah *al-Munāfiqūn* 63:9)

'God's Messenger ﷺ said, "The believing man or woman continues to have affliction in person, property and children so that they may finally meet Allah, free from sin."' (Tirmidhī)

'Set your children's eyes on piety.' (Ṭabarānī)

For those whose souls depart in childhood, life in this world is short and the journey back to God, the Eternal One is sooner than expected. Only those parents who have

gone through this know of the life-altering effects such a departure has. There are mothers and fathers with no baby in this world, yet they are parents with every cell in their body. Each one's pain and grief will differ and each parent's healing will be found in their own way. There is one promise they share, however, which is that with hardship comes ease and with *ṣabr* (forebearance), comes immense reward.

'The Prophet ﷺ was asked, "Who will be in Paradise?" He said, "Prophets will be in Paradise, martyrs will be in Paradise, infants will be in Paradise, and children buried alive will be in Paradise."' (Abū Dāwūd)

'A woman came to Allah's Messenger ﷺ and said, "O Messenger of Allah! Men (only) benefit by your teachings, so please devote to us some of your time, a day on which we may come to you so that you may teach us what Allah has taught you."

Allah's Messenger ﷺ said, "Gather on such-and-such a day at such-and-such a place." They gathered and Allah's Messenger ﷺ, came to them and taught them of what Allah had taught him. He then said, "No woman among you who has lost her three children (died) but that they will screen her from the Fire." A woman among them said, "O Allah's Messenger! If she lost two children?" She repeated her question twice, whereupon the Prophet ﷺ said, "Even two, even two, even two!"' (Bukhārī)

'The Prophet ﷺ said, "A Muslim whose three children die before the age of puberty will be granted Paradise by Allah due to His mercy for them."' (Bukhārī)

Du'ā's on Childhood

Du'ā's about childhood have two dimensions. The first is from the perspective of a child; we are all the child of someone who raised us; biological or not. Our *du'ā*'s for our parents are their right and part of our role. As children, this is one of the most significant acts of *'ibādah* (worship) we can give our parents during their life and after they leave this world: our *du'ā*'s. The second perspective is being the parent, supplicating for our child. The Prophet's tradition reminds us that a mother's *du'ā*'s for her children reserves a special place amongst those who supplicate. These *du'ā*'s encompass both of these positions, encompassing the strongest relationship.

Congratulations to a new parent:
'May Allah bless you with His gift to you,
and may you (the new parent) give thanks. May the
child reach the maturity of years, and may you be
granted its righteousness.'

Reply of the parent being congratulated
'May Allah bless you, and shower His blessings upon you,
and May Allah reward you and bestow upon you its like, and
reward you abundantly.'
(Imam al-Nawawī's *Kitāb al-Adhkār*)

*O my Sustainer! Make me one who establishes regular Prayer,
and my children too. Our Sustainer! Do accept my prayer.*
(Surah *Ibrāhīm*, 14:40)

Our Sustainer! Grant unto us spouses and offspring who will be the delight of our eyes, and make us in the forefront of those who are God-conscious. (Surah *al-Furqān* 25:74)

'O Allah, join our hearts and mend our social relationships. Guide us to the path of peace and bring us from darkness to light. Save us from obscenities, outward or inward, and bless our ears, our eyes, our hearts, our spouses and our children. And accept our repentance – indeed You are always ready to accept repentance, the ever Merciful. And make us grateful for Your blessing and make us praise it while accepting it and give it to us in full.' (Muslim)

'Allah's Messenger ﷺ taught us to say, "O Allah, make my inner nature better than my outer, and make my outer nature good. O Allah, I ask You to give me some of the abundance You give to people – in family, property and children – that neither strays nor leads astray."' (*Mishkat al-Masabih*)

Nobility in Her Nature, Courageous from Childhood

Fāṭimah al-Zahrā' 🕮: The Resplendent One
Daughter of the Noble Prophet 🕮

The Kaaba has always been central to the life of every Makkan, whether adult or child. Although the original architects, Ibrāhīm and his son Ismāʿīl 🕮, were long since forgotten by the idol-worshipping Makkans, the place was still central to the idea of 'worship'. By the beginning of the sixth century CE, in place of the sole worship of the One True God, wooden and stone statues now filled the cubic structure and rituals alien to monotheism had weaved their way all around the sacred precinct.

To the young Fāṭimah 🕮, not yet ten years old, the Kaaba was one of the familiar places to which she accompanied her father, the Prophet 🕮. Growing up in the nucleus of the nascent community, in the household of her noble parents Khadījah and Muhammad, Fāṭimah 🕮 was aware that her immediate family, unlike most of their contemporaries and relatives, were believers in God, the Creator and Sustainer of all.

Opposition from the pagan *status quo* to the noble Prophet 🕮 and his message grew. Their arrogance and narrow vested interests had created in them hardness and a lack of compassion that blinded them from the truth. The climate of hostility increased and became tenser as time went on. On one occasion, the noble Prophet 🕮, as was his wont, went to the precincts of the Kaaba to prostrate and pray to his Sustainer.

With him was his daughter Fāṭimah ﷺ. When the pagan Quraysh saw the Prophet ﷺ in prostration, they jeered at him and called for the entrails of an animal to be brought. Within moments the filth was thrown onto the noble Prophet's shoulders, whilst he was in prostration.

Fāṭimah ﷺ stood appalled as she witnessed all this. She could not bear to see her father, whom she loved so dearly, humiliated. She rushed forward to remove the filth from his shoulders and whilst doing so rebuked the Quraysh leaders for their obnoxious behaviour. Silence replaced the sound of merriment and jeering, as none of the men answered the young child. They were speechless, and it was Fāṭimah, ﷺ, who unvoiced them. Tears streamed down her face as she felt the pain and anguish, possibly more than her father.

Fāṭimah ﷺ had a very close bond with her father, as she witnessed all the tests and bitter struggles her family and believers experienced. Her sensitivity meant she was deeply affected by all that her father underwent.

The bond between herself and the noble Prophet ﷺ was more than the relationship between father and daughter. Her character was strikingly similar to his, and throughout her lifetime, even when she became a wife and mother, it was her father in whom she would confide. The Prophet ﷺ himself said of her: "Fatimah is a part of me, and whoever angers her, angers me." (Bukhari)

Of her appearance, 'Ā'ishah 🙵, the wife of the Prophet 🙵 remarked:

'I have not seen any one of God's creation resemble the messenger of God more in speech, conversation and manner of sitting than Fāṭimah, may God be pleased with her.'

Although Fāṭimah 🙵 had been blessed with children, her sincerity in the belief and practice of Islam detached her from having any attachment to the world. From her sensitive character in childhood grew an exemplary woman, as wife, mother and beloved daughter.

She worked alongside her husband, and managed the hardships – even of earning a living – that came their way. She also played an active part in supporting the Muslim community, whether it was in distributing food to the needy or providing shelter to travellers, or on the battlefield.

The worthiness of Fāṭimah 🙵, is attested by the noble Prophet 🙵 himself in the words:

'The best women in the entire world are four: Maryam, the mother of 'Isa, Khadījah, mother of the Believers, Fāṭimah, daughter of Muhammad, and Āsiyah, the wife of Pharaoh.' (Tirmidhī)

When the Prophet 🙵 gave her the news that she would be the first to leave this world after him, she laughed and looked forward to following her beloved father. At the young age of twenty-nine, Fāṭimah 🙵 passed away to the mercy of God, and was buried in Madinah.

We cause whom We will to rest in the wombs for an appointed term, then We bring you out as babies, then [nurture you] that you may reach your age of full strength (Surah *al-Ḥajj* 22:5)

Youth
Streams

Youth

Youth is the season of increasing vitality and energy. This stage is one so precious it needs to be invested in carefully before it is lost. Allah, the Guide and the Helper, has set a balance and a challenge for youth. The strengths given come hand-in-hand with responsibility and accountability.

Youth is also a testing time, especially at its onset. Initially, it is a time of transition, while you search for answers and try to define yourself. With the childhood familiarity of people and places left behind, even recognising the spectrum of one's emotions needs courage. The circles in your life are increasing, as words and actions make ripples where there were once still waters.

Far from being a time to break away from elders and their wisdom, youth is a time to move towards stable role models, and gain from their experience. It is a time to grow in maturity and understanding of your role among your family, community and humanity. It is a time when each gift one is blessed with can either be realised and channelled towards worthy goals or left useless by the wayside. Muhammad ﷺ, the noble Prophet of God, defined youth as the time up to one's fortieth year. This stage marks the meridian of life when minds can truly be thriving or be lulled to sleep with the fads and fixations that mesmerize the masses.

Streams and the journey to adulthood have much in common. Both flow with a force that makes them dynamic, cutting through mountains and forests, meeting the unexpected and changing direction – but steadily flowing on. They have the power to shape rocks and smooth stones.

The velocity of youth can be the world's best asset or become its worst threat. Yet streams and young adulthood are home to an array of beauty and varieties of life, as their scenes and landscapes change. Eventually, they find their way downhill and meander towards the sea merging into its waves. As they gain momentum, young lives too move on to the larger world of possibilities.

Myriad Voices

'Fortunate am I to receive the treasures of youth.
Time delivers the gifts of strength, health and opportunity,
to cultivate mind and soul.
O Most Bounteous, lead me to use these gifts
To please You
The Source of all Goodness, the Protecting Friend.'

'I stand on ground that shifts daily between childhood and
adulthood. With one foot in each place I need stability,
reassurance and the friendship and guidance of my guardians.'

'All
I really
want
is to be
understood.'

'I don't intend to make anyone's life hard, be disruptive or
cause pain. I need to learn how and when to express myself.
My emotions may overwhelm you. They frighten me too and
I struggle to direct and harness all that I say and feel.

I have the energy and enthusiasm to achieve my goals and
I need help to navigate when the course in not straight; help

to regain my foothold when I falter; help to find a way when feeling trapped.

Shown where to plant, I can sow my seeds, and labour well. Then when the time comes to reap, I will find contentment with my work and satisfaction to those around me.'

'Sometimes I wish I could just fly away from all the inspection, questions and suspicion. I have done nothing wrong, yet the wrongs of my contemporaries are piled up high and used to break me down.

Why am I not seen as "Me"?
I wish I could fly away, stretch my wings and soar through the sky and use my God-given energy in a flight up into the open welcoming sky.'

'From the outside, my cocoon may not look likeable. It is awkward, not "fitting in" to the norms of the outside world. My habitat, this cocoon, is delicate. Yet beneath the thin skin, a miracle is taking place. My wings are forming, and if the right conditions prevail, one day soon I will metamorphose and emerge as an individual. My wings will be strong enough to ride the winds and rise above branches as I grace the leaves with my unique and distinct patterns.

But first, I need to be fed and nurtured carefully. Each change has its own special time, and when my time comes, I hope my wings will be strong enough to carry me through all weathers as I join the landscape of the world.'

'Who am *I* really?
At home I fulfil all their wishes, say what they want to hear,
read and watch what they don't mind much.
Outside I step into a different me – what I say, what I see,
what I think – I am free.
Or am I an echo? A shadow of my friends?
Hear what they hear,
Say what they say,
See what they see,
Think what they…
– do I think?
Am *I* me?'

The Eternal Sources

Every stage of life is a valued gift to cherish. The blessings of health and time should be used to grow to one's full potential, reaching out to opportunities that come along the way.

It is God Who created you in a state of [helpless] weakness, then gave [you] strength after weakness, then, after strength, gave [you] weakness and a hoary head: He creates whatever He wills, and it is He Who has all knowledge and power. (Surah *al-Rūm* 30:54)

'God's Messenger ﷺ said: "Grasp five things before five others: your youth before your old age, your health before your illness, your riches before your poverty, your leisure before your work, and your life before your death."' (Tirmidhī)

'The Prophet ﷺ said: "On the Day of Resurrection the feet of the son of Adam will not move away till he is questioned about five matters: on what did he spend his life; in doing what he made his youth pass away; from where did he acquire his wealth; on what did he spend it, and what did he do with his knowledge."' (Tirmidhī)

'The Prophet ﷺ said: "Allah will give shade to seven on the day when there will be no shade but His." Among the seven persons is "a youth who has been brought up in the worship of Allah" – that is, he has worshipped Allah sincerely from childhood.' (Bukhārī)

The world is rich in treasures to discover and learn about. There are a multitude of people with different opinions and contrasting backgrounds, new ideas which lead to countless directions. Finding your direction requires honesty, courage and integrity. Society around you may redefine its values every few years: what was admirable yesterday is mocked today. Living by your values needs a timeless strength and confidence in something greater than inconsistent opinions.

It is not righteousness that you turn your faces towards the east or the west;
but [true] righteousness is to believe in God and the Last Day, and the Angels, and the Book, and the Messengers;
to spend of your wealth, despite your love of it, for your kin, for orphans, for the needy, for the wayfarer, for those who ask, and for the ransom of slaves;
to be steadfast in Prayer, and practice regular charity;
to fulfil the contracts that you have made;
and, to be firm and patient, in pain and suffering and adversity, and throughout all periods of panic.
Such are the people of truth, the God-fearing.
(Surah *al-Baqarah* 2:177)

And so, set your face steadfastly towards the one ever-true faith, turning away from all that is false, in accordance with the natural disposition which God has instilled into human beings. Not to allow any change to corrupt what God has thus created – this is [the purpose of the one] ever-true faith. (Surah *al-Rūm* 30:30)

Those who turn [to Allah] in repentance; who serve Him, and praise Him; who wander in devotion to the cause of Allah; who

*bow down and prostrate themselves in Prayer; who enjoin good
and forbid evil; and observe the limits set by Allah. So proclaim
the glad tidings to such believers.* (Surah *al-Tawbah* 9:112)

'God's Messenger ﷺ neither talked in an insulting manner nor
did he ever speak evil intentionally. He used to say,
"The most beloved to me among you is the one who has
the best character and manners."' (Bukhārī)

I hastened to You, O my Sustainer, that You might be pleased.
(Surah *Tā Hā* 20:84)

'The Prophet ﷺ said, "There is nothing heavier than
good character put in the scale of a believer on the Day of
Resurrection."' (Abū Dāwūd)

**Through the grace of God – who is *al-Hādī*, the Guide,
and *al-Mujīb*, the Responsive – we seek His help to
develop the characteristics which attains harmony in this
life and everlasting success in the next. Whichever way
we take a step, our faith is our reference point, our centre,
from which ripples the rest of our life.**

*For all men and women who submit to God,
for all men and women who believe in God,
for all devout men and women,
for all true men and women,
for all men and women who are patient and constant,
for all men and women who humble themselves,
for all men and women who give in charity,
for all men and women who fast [and control themselves],*

for all men and women who guard their chastity,
and for all men and women who engage much in God's
remembrance: for them has God prepared forgiveness and great
reward. (Surah *al-Aḥzāb* 33:35)

Those who believe, and do deeds of righteousness, and establish
regular Prayer and regular charity, will have their reward with
their Sustainer: on them shall be no fear, nor shall they grieve.
(Surah *al-Baqarah* 2:277)

By no means shall you attain righteousness unless you give [freely]
of that which you love; and whatever you give, of a truth God
knows it well. (Surah *Āl 'Imrān* 3:92)

Your Sustainer knows best what is in your hearts: If you do
deeds of righteousness, He is certainly most Forgiving to those
who turn to Him again and again [in true penitence].
(Surah *Banī Isrā'īl* 17:25)

'The Prophet ﷺ said: "Nothing is weightier in the scales of
a believer on the Day of Judgment than his good behaviour.
Allah treats with displeasure a person who is given to loose and
vulgar talk."' (Tirmidhī)

'God's Messenger ﷺ said: "If you have four characteristics,
whatever worldly advantage passes you by does not benefit
you: keeping a trust, speaking the truth, a good character, and
moderation in food."' (Aḥmad)

'God's Messenger ﷺ said: "Do not speak much without
mentioning Allah, for much talk without the mention of Allah
produces hardness of heart, and the one who is farthest from
Allah is he who has a hard heart."' (Tirmidhī)

Say: 'Not equal are things that are bad and things that are good,
even though the abundance of the bad may dazzle you.
So fear Allah, O you that understand, that you may prosper.'
(Surah *al-Mā'idah* 5:100)

A stable character is one where knowledge and actions
work in unison to strengthen one's faith. This character
is rooted in the timeless virtues of humility, patience
and fortitude.

Who is better in speech than one who calls [people] to God,
acts righteously, and says: 'I am of those who submit to God.'
(Surah *Fuṣṣilāt* 41:33)

Only those believe in Our signs [āyāt] who, when they are
reminded of them, fall down in prostration, and glorify the praises
of their Sustainer, and they are not proud. Their sides forsake
their beds [at night] as they call upon their Sustainer in fear [of
punishment and Hell fire] and hope [of reward and Paradise],
and they spend [in charity] out of what We have bestowed on
them. (Surah *al-Sajdah* 32:15–16)

Those who show patience, firmness and self-control; who are true
[in word and deed]; who worship devoutly; who spend [in the way
of God]; and who pray for forgiveness in the early hours of the
morning. (Surah *Āl 'Imrān* 3:17)

And they fall down on their faces weeping and it adds to their
humility. (Surah *Banī Isrā'īl* 17:109)

They used to sleep but little by night [calling upon their Sustainer and praying, with fear and hope]. And in the hours before dawn, they were [found] asking [Allah] for forgiveness, and in their wealth and possessions there was a right for the one who asks and the [needy person] prevented [from asking].
(Surah *al-Dhāriyāt* 51:17–19)

On those who believe and work deeds of righteousness, will [God] Most Gracious bestow love. (Surah *Maryam* 19:96)

Guiding the soul is the key to a lasting good character. The best direction for the soul is in the remembrance of God and virtuous actions. We are never alone in our efforts, for God is *al-Wālī* – The Protecting Friend.

Whoever does good benefits his own soul; whoever does evil, it is against his own soul. Nor is thy Sustainer ever unjust [in the least] to His Servants. (Surah *Fuṣṣilāt* 41:46)

We bestowed wisdom on Luqmān, [enjoining]: 'Show gratitude to God.' Any who is [so] grateful does so to the profit of his own soul. But if any is ungrateful, God is indeed free of all wants, worthy of all praise. (Surah *Luqmān* 31:12)

Whoever submits his whole self to God, and is a doer of good, has grasped indeed the most trustworthy hand-hold: and with God rests the end and decision of [all] affairs. (Surah *Luqmān* 31:32)

O you who believe! Fear Allah and keep your duty to Him. And let every person look to what he has sent forth for the morrow,

and fear Allah. Indeed, Allah is All-Aware of whatever you do.
(Surah *al-Ḥashr* 59:18)

'Allah's Messenger ﷺ said: "Indeed, Allah likes three things for
you and He disapproves of three things for you.

He is pleased with you that you worship Him and associate
not anything with Him, that you hold fast to the rope of Allah,
and be not scattered; and He disapproves of your irrelevant
talk, persistent questioning and the wasting of wealth.'"
(Muslim)

'Religion is very easy and whoever overburdens himself in
his religion will not be able to continue in that way. So you
should not be extremists, but try to be near to perfection'.
(Bukhārī).

'The Prophet ﷺ was asked: "Which deed is most beloved to
Allah?" He said, "The one that is done regularly, even if it is
little."' (Bukhārī)

'Allah's Messenger ﷺ entered the mosque and a person
followed him. The man prayed and went to the Prophet ﷺ
and greeted him. The Prophet ﷺ returned the greeting and
said to him, "Go back and pray, for you have not prayed."
The man went back, prayed in the same way as before,
returned and greeted the Prophet ﷺ, who said: "Go back and
pray, for you have not prayed." This happened three times.
The man said, "By Him Who sent you with the Truth, I
cannot offer the prayer in a better way than this. Please, teach
me how to pray." The Prophet ﷺ said, "When you stand
for Prayer, say God is Most Great – *Allāhu Akbar* – and then
recite from the Holy Qur'an (of what you know by heart) and

then bow till you feel at ease. Then raise your head and stand up straight, then prostrate till you feel at ease during your prostration, then sit with calmness till you feel at ease (do not hurry) and do the same in all your Prayers."' (Bukhārī)

As youth grows, so do our relationships. In the zeal and speed of life, we should invest in our relationships as we do in other areas of our life. Good character extends to respecting those around us: our relatives, the young and old, those whom we know, and those we do not.

We enjoined upon man to be dutiful to his parents: in travail upon travail did his mother bear him, and in years twain was his weaning. [Hear the command]: 'Show gratitude to Me and to your parents: to Me is [the final] Goal.' (Surah *Luqmān* 31:14)

Your [real] friends are [no less than] God, His Messenger, and the [fellowship of] believers – those who establish regular Prayer and regular charity, and bow down humbly [in worship].
As to those who turn [for friendship] to God, His Messenger, and the [fellowship of] believers, it is the party of Allah that must certainly triumph. (Surah *al-Māʾidah* 5:55–56)

The believing men and women, are associates and helpers of one another. They [join together] to promote all that is beneficial and discourage all that is evil; to establish Prayer and give charity, and to obey God and His Messenger. Those are the people whom God would grant mercy. Indeed God is Almighty and All Wise. (Surah *al-Tawbah* 9:71)

'Narrated 'Ā'ishah (☺): "I heard the Prophet (☺) say, 'Souls are like recruited troops: Those who have like qualities are inclined to each other, but those who have dissimilar qualities, differ.'" (Bukhārī)

'The Prophet ☺ said: "Whoever believes in Allah and the Last Day should not hurt his neighbour; and whoever believes in Allah and the Last Day should serve his guest generously; and whoever believes in Allah and the Last Day should say what is good or keep quiet."' (Bukhārī)

'God's Messenger ☺ said: "No youth will honour an old man because of his years without God appointing one to honour him when he is old."' (Tirmidhī)

'I heard al-Bara' ibn 'Azib saying: "The Prophet ☺ orders us to do seven things and prohibited us from doing seven other things." Then al-Bara' mentioned the following: " To pay a visit to the sick, to follow funeral processions, to say to one who sneezes, 'May Allah be merciful to you', to return greetings, to help the oppressed, to accept invitations, and to help others to fulfil their oaths."' (Bukhārī)

'Abū Hurayrah reported: "The Prophet ☺ said, 'Wealth is not in having many possessions. Rather, true wealth is the richness of the soul.'" (Muslim)

This is a stage of life where there is constant building: interests, projects, causes, careers, friendships, new homes, distant vistas beyond the horizon. Underpinning this activity with noble intentions elevates the simplest act into

an act of worship. Allah – *al-Samī*, the All Hearing, al-*Baṣīr*, the All Seeing – rewards every good.

Whoever acts righteously, male or female, and has faith, We will certainly give him a new life, a life that is good and pure and We will bestow on such their reward according to the best of their actions. (Surah *al-Naḥl* 16:97)

If any do deeds of righteousness – be they male or female – and has faith, they will enter Paradise, and not the least injustice will be done to them. (Surah *al-Nisā'* 4:124)

But those who believe and act righteously, and humble themselves before their Sustainer – they will be companions of Paradise, to dwell therein forever! (Surah *Hūd* 11:23)

And whoever of you is devout in the service of God and His Messenger, and does good, We shall grant her reward twice; and We have prepared for her a generous sustenance. (Surah *al-Aḥzāb* 33:31)

But those who believe and did righteous deeds, and believe in the [Revelation] sent down to Muhammad – for it is the Truth from their Sustainer – He will remove from them their ills and improve their condition. (Surah *Muhammad* 47:2)

But those who believe and do righteous deeds, We shall soon admit them to Gardens, through which rivers flow – to dwell therein forever: Therein they shall have companions pure and We shall admit them to shelter with cool and ever deepening shade. (Surah *al-Nisā'* 4:57)

'Allah's Messenger ﷺ said: "There is in Paradise an apartment, the exterior of which can be seen from its interior, and the interior of which can be seen from its exterior. Such apartments have been prepared for those who are polite in talk, provide food (to the needy), fast frequently and observe the Tahajjud Prayer when people are asleep."' (Aḥmad)

'The Prophet ﷺ said: " If you guarantee me six things on your part I shall guarantee you Paradise:
Speak the truth when you talk,
keep a promise when you make it,
when you are trusted with something fulfil your trust,
avoid sexual immorality,
lower your gaze, and restrain your hands from injustice."'
(Aḥmad)

Duʿāʾ's to Strengthen and Guide

These *duʿāʾ*'s ask for strength and guidance, especially as one's youth is a time of decision-making and finding one's path. These *duʿāʾ*'s are about recognizing priorities. Sometimes, in this phase of life, the speed of changing emotions makes it hard to know what to make *duʿāʾ* for: heart, mind, soul, and people's opinions, pull us in a thousand ways. In the midst of all the noise, external and internal, it's these *duʿāʾ*'s that stand out for a traveller; a guiding brightness from a constellation on a lonely night, to show the way.

Our Sustainer! Grant us good in this world and good in the life to come and keep us safe from the torment of the Fire.
(Surah *al-Baqarah* 2:201)

Our Sustainer! Bestow on us endurance and make our foothold sure and give us help against those who reject faith.
(Surah *al-Baqarah* 2:250)

Our Sustainer! Behold, we have heard a voice calling us unto faith saying, 'Believe in your Sustainer' and we have believed.
(Surah *Āl ʿImrān* 3:193)

Our Sustainer! Pour out on us patience and constancy, and make us die as those who have surrendered themselves unto You.
(Surah *al-Aʿrāf* 7:126)

Our Sustainer! Bestow on us mercy from Your presence and dispose of our affairs for us in the right way.
(Surah *al-Kahf* 18:10)

Our Sustainer! Forgive us our sins as well as those of our brethren who proceeded us in faith and let not our hearts entertain any unworthy thoughts or feelings against [any of] those who have believed. Our Sustainer! You are indeed full of kindness and Most Merciful. (Surah *al-Ḥashr* 59:10)

Our Sustainer! Perfect our light for us and forgive us our sins, for indeed You have power over all things. (Surah *al-Taḥrīm* 66:8)

'O Allah, help me in remembering You, in being grateful to You, in worshipping You in an excellent manner.'
(Abū Dāwūd)

'Umm Darda reported: "My husband reported that he heard Allah's Messenger (ﷺ) as saying: 'He who supplicates for his brother behind his back (in his absence), the Angel commissioned (for carrying supplication to his Lord) says: "Amen, and it is for you also"'." (Muslim)

Exemplary In Her Independence, Influential Through Her Courage

Asmā' ﷺ, daughter of Abū Bakr ﷺ

In the endless blur of sand which characterises the desert land of the Ḥijāz, punctuated by the mountain ranges, a most significant journey was about to take place: the Hijrah of the Prophet Muhammad ﷺ and his friend Abu Bakr ﷺ. This covert departure from the city of Makkah to the city of Light and Hope, Madinah, was both dangerous and life-threatening for all the believers involved. Asmā', ﷺ played a key role in their plans.

Asmā' ﷺ, the young daughter of Abū Bakr ﷺ, was the eighteenth person in Makkah to accept the final Messenger of God ﷺ as a Prophet and Islam as her faith. Now at the age of twenty-seven, her independence and courage were instrumental time and again in the development of the Muslim community.

On the night of her father and the noble Prophet's departure, Asmā' ﷺ was responsible for providing food and water for them. She famously tore her waistband in two to secure the supplies for them, giving her the title of the 'one with two waistbands'.

After their departure, staying in Makkah itself was, for the remaining believers, oppressive and difficult. When Asmā's non-believing grandfather came to visit her father's home, enquiring about his whereabouts and what he had left for their upkeep, Asmā' ﷺ displayed her quick thinking. She took the blind elderly man's hands to a ledge in the wall and lay them on a cloth covering some pebbles. 'My father has left abundant wealth,' she said, forestalling any further charges made about her beloved father as well as avoiding any need to accept money from her grandfather.

Asmā' ؓ left Makkah a short time after Abū Bakr ؓ and the Prophet ﷺ. Her pregnancy did not deter her and she made the journey amidst the sand swirling winds, dunes and rocky ridges. So advanced was her stage of pregnancy that she gave birth before reaching Madinah in a settlement on its outskirts called Qubā, the landmark where the Prophet ﷺ stopped to build the first mosque. Her son was the first to be born in the Islamic calendar, which began on the year of the Prophet's migration. His name was 'Abdullāh ؓ, and he was in the vanguard of the Muslims' struggle and cause.

The life of Asmā' ؓ was characterised by financial hardship and physical trials. She worked alongside her husband by drawing water, transporting grain and caring for the limited livestock in their possession. Yet, her generosity was renowned and she gave to those less fortunate than herself without measure. Even when she inherited an orchard from her sister 'Ā'ishah ؓ, she sold it and distributed the money to those in need.

The courage and strength of her youth did not diminish with age. Asmā's biography travels from one event of courage to another. Like many other Companions of the Prophet ﷺ she shouldered responsibilities from a young age, and became an asset in creating a strong community.

Knowledge
Springs

And if all the trees on earth were pens and the ocean [were ink], with seven oceans behind it to add to its [supply], yet the words of Allah would not be exhausted [in the writing]: for Allah is Exalted in Power, full of Wisdom.
(Surah *Luqmān* 31:27)

Knowledge

The Qur'an invites each of us, throughout our life, to seek knowledge that will bring us to understand our past, our future, the world and ourselves. Thinking, reflecting, searching and pondering are the most basic of human obligations and rights.

The pursuit of knowledge is an obligation we owe to ourselves. After all, how can one be truly alive without contemplating our surroundings? How can we greet each new day and all that it brings, be a part of the moving spectacle of planets and stars, witness the magnificent display in the sky, and not want to know more about our part and purpose in it all? Knowledge, in its broadest sense, is not limited to the boxes separating the sacred and secular. We know that the first Prophet of God, Adam ﷺ, was taught the name of all things, thus encompassing languages and the vast workings of this world; this is all knowledge.

Your education started before you entered this world. In the womb you learnt of changes through sounds, smell and taste, and knew the difference between light and dark. Your mother's emotions directly informed you of feelings in your minute world. As your limbs took shape you absorbed more of the environment. Your education had begun and you were being initiated into a world of 'knowing'.

As rites of passage go, the new-born is welcomed into the world with '*Allāhu Akbar*... God is Most Great, *Allāhu Akbar*... God is Most Great', followed by the testimony of faith. These words form the bedrock of our journey 'to know' on earth; they remind us of our place in relation to *al-Alīm* – the All Knowing.

Gaining knowledge can follow many avenues: from sitting at the feet of grandparents and elders, or in lecture theatres in prestigious institutions. Whichever route we take, real knowledge should open our hearts and minds to recognize how awe-inspiring the universe is. Real knowledge will elevate our soul, and bring humility and God-consciousness. It brings self-respect and the power to live by the truth.

Knowledge which affirms the truth is a life force. Similarly, springs, in all their different shapes and origins, are the source of much pure water. They emanate from the earth, just as we humans do; they provide a life source to their surroundings, in the same way a person with knowledge does. Springs and knowledge are vital to life.

Myriad Voices

'As I embark on years of further education, I need to ask myself
what it is for?
What am I devoting my best and fittest years to?
How will my study be of benefit to those around me?
Are my eyes set solely on personal gains?
Will my knowledge contribute to my role as a custodian of this
earth, will it contribute to my benefit in the hereafter?
With my purpose clear, I begin.'

'A part of me envies babies. When did I lose the fearless thirst
"to know"? They see no obstacle in their search to understand
their surroundings, no barriers, no introspection, no self
reproaching. They simply get on with the job of 'finding out'.
What I would give to have their courage again!'

'"Congratulations", they said, "You've graduated.""But into
what?" I thought.
Into arrogance, prejudice and conceit? Into an elitist
clique, that peers down, dictating from lofty towers to the
"uneducated" and taking pride in theorizing and hypothesizing,
postulating and pretending to 'know' about things they don't
really understand?
Yes, I had graduated, but I hoped not into any of that.'

'In the lonely eternity which is now my home,
I thank my friend Knowledge for staying by my side.
As the worldly life has passed away,
Everything else is left behind.
All I take with me are the actions and deeds
That grew from our companionship.
The light from that learning shines on,
Here on the other side.

Here on the other side
The light from that learning shines on,
That grew from our companionship.
All I take with me are the actions and deeds
Everything else is left behind.
As the worldly life has passed away,
I thank my friend Knowledge for staying by my side.
In the lonely eternity which is now my home.'

'How often have I told my child they'll understand more when they're older?
Now I watch humbled at what true 'knowing' really is.
As they pour over seeds and soil and water their plants with such care, they are confident and trusting in the unseen.
They inform me their plants will shoot out of the deep, black hole in the ground "when Allah decides". I see true knowledge evident in the fertile minds of children who have understood faith already.'

The Eternal Sources

**At the foundation of all learning, we know that God –
al-Alīm, the All-Knowing, *al-Ḥakim*, the Most Wise –
is the source of all knowledge, past, present and future.
The seen and the unseen, all knowledge lies with
Him alone.**

*Allah! There is no god but He, the Ever Living, the Self-subsisting,
Eternal. No drowsiness can seize Him, nor sleep. To Him
belongs whatever is in the heavens and on earth. Who is there to
intercede in His presence except as He permits? He knows what
[appears to His creatures as] before or behind them. Nor shall they
encompass any of His knowledge except as He wills. His throne of
almightiness extends over the heavens and the earth, and He feels
no fatigue in guarding and preserving them, for He is the Most
High, the Supreme [in glory].* (Surah *al-Baqarah* 2:255)

*He is the First and the Last, the Evident and the Hidden:
and He has full knowledge of all things.* (Surah *al-Ḥadīd* 57:3)

*He merges night into day, and He merges day into night;
and He has full knowledge of the secrets of [all] hearts.*
(Surah *al-Ḥadīd* 57:6)

*Do you not see that God knows [all] that is in the heavens and
on earth? There is not a secret consultation between three, but
He is the fourth of them, or between five but He is the sixth, nor
between fewer or more, but He is with them, wheresoever they
may be: In the end He will tell them what they did on the
Day of Judgment. For Allah has full knowledge of all things.*
(Surah *al-Mujādalah* 58:7)

It is He Who has created for you all things that are on earth;
Moreover, His design comprehended the heavens, for He gave
order and perfection to the seven heavens. And of all things
He has perfect knowledge. (Surah *al-Baqarah* 2:29)

**If we sincerely seek to understand and use our intellect,
we will use wisdom and guidance to lead us in the
right direction.**

We have sent among you a Messenger from yourselves, reciting to
you Our signs, purifying you, and instructing you in the scripture
and wisdom, and in new knowledge. So remember Me; I will
remember you all. Be grateful to Me, and do not reject or be
ungrateful to Me. (Surah *al-Baqarah* 2:151–152)

It is He who sends down clear messages to His servant to bring you
out of darknesses into the light. Allah is All-Gentle with you, ever
Merciful. (Surah *al-Ḥadīd* 57:9)

He it is Who has sent down to you the Book. In it are verses basic
or fundamental [of established meaning]; they are the foundation
of the Book. Others are allegorical. Those in whose hearts is
perversity follow the part thereof that is allegorical, seeking discord,
and searching for its hidden meanings, although none knows
its hidden meanings except Allah. And those who are firmly
grounded in knowledge say: 'We believe in the Book; the whole
of it is from our Sustainer:' None will grasp the Message except
people of understanding. (Surah *Āl ʿImrān* 3:7)

There is no god but He: that is the witness of Allah, His angels,
and those endowed with knowledge, standing firm on justice.

There is no god but He, the Exalted in Power, the Wise.
(Surah Āl ʿImrān 3:18)

*It is He who takes your souls by night, and has knowledge of all
that you have done by day, then by day He raises you up again so
that the term appointed by Him is fulfilled. In the end unto Him
will be your return, then will He show you the truth of all that
you did.* (Surah al-Anʿām 6:60)

**God is *al-Laṭīf*, the Subtle One, and *al-Wāsiʿ*, the All
Pervading, with whom lies the secrets and the knowledge
of the unseen.**

*Say, O Prophet: 'I have no power over any good or harm to myself
except as Allah wills. If I had knowledge of the Unseen, I should
have secured for myself an abundance of wealth, and no evil
should have touched me: I am only a warner, and a bringer of
glad tidings to those who have faith.'* (Surah al-Aʿrāf 7:188)

*With Him are the keys of the Unseen, the treasures that none
knows but He. He knows whatever there is on the earth and in
the sea; not a leaf falls but with His knowledge. There is not a
grain in the darkness [or depths] of the earth, nor anything moist
or dry [alive or dead], that has not been inscribed in a Clear
Record.* (Surah al-Anʿām 6:59)

*The knowledge of the Hour is indeed with God [alone]. It is He
Who sends down rain, and He Who knows what is in the wombs.
Nor does anyone know what it is that he will earn on the morrow:
nor does anyone know in what land he is to die. With God indeed
is full knowledge and He is acquainted [with all things].*
(Surah Luqmān 31:34)

'The Prophet ﷺ said, "The keys of the unseen are five and none knows them but Allah: None knows what is in the womb, but Allah; none knows what will happen tomorrow, but Allah; none knows when it will rain, but Allah; none knows where he will die, but Allah; and none knows when the Hour will happen, but Allah."' (Bukhārī)

Seeking knowledge is an obligation upon every person, male and female. Knowing the truth about our Sustainer, about our world, and about ourselves, is indeed a basic human right. True growth comes from knowing. Hence we are instructed to read, think and reflect.

Read in the name of your Sustainer Who created man from a [fertilised ovum] clinging [to the uterus].
Read and your Sustainer is Most Generous,
Who taught the use of the pen,
taught man what he knew not.
But, man most surely transgresses,
because he sees himself as self-sufficient.
Surely to your Sustainer is the return. (Surah *al-'Alaq* 96:1–8)

God sets forth parables for humankind that they may take heed. (Surah *Ibrāhīm* 14:25)

Such are the parables which We put forward to people that they may reflect. (Surah *al-Ḥashr* 59:21)

Indeed, We created man to toil and struggle. (Surah *al-Balad* 90:4)

*In the creation of the heavens and the earth, and in the
alternation of night and day, there are indeed signs for people
with understanding – those who remember Allah standing,
sitting, and lying down on their sides, and think deeply about the
creation of the heavens and the earth and say: 'Our Sustainer!
You have not created this in vain! Glory to You!'*
(Surah *Āl 'Imrān* 3:190–191)

**The benefits of seeking knowledge are manifold for
those who venture forth. It is knowledge that gives us
hope in the future, knowledge which informs choices,
knowledge which carves a moral framework; ultimately it
is knowledge which leads to success in both worlds.**

*[God makes clear] that those who have been given knowledge may
learn that the [Qur'an] is the Truth from your Sustainer, and
that they may believe therein, and that their hearts may submit
to it with humility. And indeed God is the Guide of those who
believe to the Straight Way.* (Surah *al-Ḥajj* 22:54)

*Do they not travel through the land, so that their hearts [and
minds] may thus learn wisdom and their ears may thus learn to
hear? Truly it is not their eyes that are blind, but the hearts in
their breasts.* (Surah *al-Ḥajj* 22:46)

'No people sit together remembering Allah, but the angels
surround them, mercy envelops them, tranquillity descends
upon them, and Allah mentions them to those who are in
His presence.' (Muslim)

'God's Messenger ﷺ said: "One who goes out to search for knowledge is (devoted) to the cause of God till he returns."' (Tirmidhī)

'Acquiring knowledge in company for an hour in the night is better than spending the whole night in prayer.' (Al-Muttaqī al-Hindī, *Kanz al-ʿummāl*)

'ʿĀʾishah ﷺ praised the women of Anṣār for their spirit of enquiry and learning, saying, "How praiseworthy are the women of Anṣār that their modesty does not prevent them from attempts at learning and the acquisition of knowledge."' (Muslim)

The pursuit of knowledge leads one in many directions. When looking for the truth, it is essential to know Our Sustainer, His books, Prophets and the guidance with which they were sent.

Those to whom We gave the Book recite and follow it as it should be recited and followed; they are the ones who believe in it. Those who disbelieve in it, they are the losers. (Surah *al-Baqarah* 2:121)

God has revealed from time to time the most beautiful message in the form of a Book, consistent with itself [yet] repeating [its teaching in various aspects]… (Surah *al-Zumar* 39:23)

We have given all kinds of examples to people in this Qurʾan so that hopefully they will take heed. [It is] a Qurʾan in Arabic with

no distortion, so that hopefully they will attain God-consciousness.
(Surah *al-Zumar* 39:27–28)

When the Qur'an is read, listen to it with attention, and hold
your peace so that you may receive God's grace and mercy.
(Surah *al-A'rāf* 7:204)

Those who follow the Messenger, the unlettered Prophet, whom
they find mentioned in their own [scriptures] – the Torah and the
Gospel – for he commands them what is good and forbids them
what is evil. He allows them as lawful what is wholesome and
pure and prohibits them from what is bad and impure; he releases
them from their heavy burdens and from the yokes that are upon
them. So it is those who believe in him, honour him, help him,
and follow the light which is sent down with him – it is they who
will prosper.

Say: 'O people! I am sent unto you all, as the Messenger of Allah,
to Whom belongs the dominion of the heavens and the earth.
There is no god but He. It is He Who gives both life and death.
So believe in Allah and His Messenger, the unlettered Prophet,
who believes in Allah and His words. Follow him that you may
be guided.' (Surah *al-A'rāf* 7:157–158)

From knowledge springs virtuous actions and intentions,
this is the essence of true understanding.

And remember, [O Prophet], your Sustainer in your [very] soul,
with humility and in reverence, and without loudness in words,
in the mornings and evenings. And do not be of those who
are heedless.

Those who are near to your Sustainer, are not too proud to worship Him; they celebrate His praises, and prostrate before Him. (Surah *al-Aʿrāf* 7:205–206)

But those among them who are well-grounded in knowledge and the believers, they believe in what has been revealed to you [O Muhammad] and what was revealed before you. And [especially] those who establish regular Prayer and give the purifying tax [Zakat] and believe in Allah and in the Last Day, to them We shall give a great reward. (Surah *al-Nisāʾ* 4:162)

Say [O Muhammad]: 'The things that my Sustainer has indeed forbidden are: shameful deeds, whether open or secret; sins and trespasses against truth or reason; assigning of partners to Allah, for which He has given no authority; and saying things about Allah of which you have no knowledge.' (Surah *al-Aʿrāf* 7:33)

O you who believe! Ask not questions about things which, if made plain to you, may cause you trouble. But if you ask about things when the Qur'an is being revealed, they will be made plain to you. Allah will forgive those, for He is Oft-forgiving, Most Forbearing. Some people before you did ask such questions, and on that account became ungrateful rejecters of the truth. (Surah *al-Māʾidah* 5:101–102)

'Allah's Messenger ﷺ said: "The knowledge from which no benefit is derived is like a treasure out of which nothing is spent in the cause of Allah."' (Aḥmad)

For those who wish to learn with their hearts and minds, the whole earth is laid open, replete with the astonishing signs of God.

*It is He who sends down water from the sky. From it you drink
and from it come the vegetation on which you graze your herds.
And by it He makes crops grow for you and olives and dates and
grapes and fruit of every kind. There is certainly a sign in that for
people who reflect.*

*He has made the night and the day subservient to you, and the sun,
the moon and the stars are all subject to His command.
There are certainly signs in that for people who use their intellect.
And also the things of varying colours He has created for you in
the earth. There is certainly a sign in that for people who
pay heed.*

*It is He who made the sea subservient to you so that you can eat
fresh and tender meat from it and bring out from it ornaments
to wear. And you see the ships cleaving through it so that you can
seek His bounty, and so that perhaps you may show thanks.
He cast firmly embedded mountains on the earth so it would not
move under you, and rivers and pathways so that perhaps you may
be guided. And landmarks and the stars by which people
are guided.*

*Is He Who creates like the one who does not create? Will you not
then pay heed?* (Surah *al-Naḥl* 16:10–17)

*Do you not see that God has subjected to you everything in the
heavens and earth and has showered His blessings upon you, both
outwardly and inwardly? Yet there are people who argue about
God without knowledge or guidance or any illuminating Book.*
(Surah *Luqmān* 31:20)

Say, 'Travel through the earth and see the final fate of the deniers.'
(Surah *al-An'ām* 6:11)

Ask them: 'Are those who know equal to those who do not know?'
(Surah *al-Zumar* 39:9)

**Learning which is infused with God consciousness is part
of a balanced lifestyle. We are reminded of taking the
middle path in all aspects of our lives.**

*[O Prophet], your Sustainer knows that you stand [for Prayer]
nigh two-thirds of the night, or half the night, or a third of the
night, and so do a party of those with you.*

*But Allah appoints the night and day in due measure. He knows
that you are unable to keep count thereof. So He has turned to you
[in mercy].*

*Read, then, of the Qur'an as much as may be easy for you.
He knows that there may be [some] among you in ill-health,
others travelling through the land, seeking of God's bounty,
and yet others fighting in God's cause. Read, therefore, as much
of the Qur'an as may be easy [for you], and establish regular
Prayer and give Zakat, and give to God a beautiful loan.
And whatever good you send forth for yourselves, you shall find
it with God. That is better and greater in reward. And seek the
grace of God, for indeed God is Oft-Forgiving, ever Merciful.*
(Surah *al-Muzzammil*, 73:20)

'Ḥanẓalah al-Usaydī, (a Companion of the Prophet ﷺ) said:
"I met Abū Bakr, and he asked me, 'How are you, O Ḥanẓalah?'

I said, 'Ḥanẓalah has become a *munāfiq* (hypocrite).'
He said, '*SubḥānAllāh* – Glory be to God! What are you saying?'

I said, 'We sit with the Messenger of Allah ﷺ and he tells us about Hell and Paradise until it is as if we can see them. Then when we leave the Messenger of Allah ﷺ, we get involved with our wives and children and earning a living, and we forget a lot.'

Abū Bakr said, 'I feel the same way.' So Abū Bakr and I went to the Messenger of Allah ﷺ, and I said, 'Ḥanẓalah has become a hypocrite, O Messenger of Allah.'

"The Messenger of Allah ﷺ said: 'Why is that?'
I said, 'O Messenger of Allah, we sit with you and you tell us about Hell and Paradise until it is as if we can see them. Then when we leave you, we get involved with our wives and children and earning a living, and we forget a lot.'

"The Messenger of Allah ﷺ said, 'By the One in Whose hand is my soul, if you continued to be as you are when you are with me, and to make *dhikr*, the angels would shake your hands in your beds and on the road. But, O Ḥanẓalah, there is a time for this and a time for that' and he said this three times.'" (Muslim)

Seeking knowledge with the intention of pleasing our Sustainer and hoping for His blessings turns all endeavours into acts of worship and brings us closer to Him.

It is only those who have knowledge among His servants who fear Allah. (Surah *Fāṭir* 35:28)

'Allah's Messenger ﷺ said: "He whom death overtakes while he is engaged in acquiring knowledge with a view to reviving Islam with the help of it, there will be one degree between him and the Prophets in Paradise."' (*Sunan* al-Dārimī)

'The Prophet ﷺ said: "A servant of Allah will remain standing on the Day of Judgment till he is questioned about his youth and how he spent it; and about his knowledge and how he utilized it; about his wealth from where he acquired it and in what (activities) he spent it; and about his body and how he used it."' (Tirmidhī)

'He added: "Allah, His angels and all those in heavens and on earth, even the ants in their hills and the fish in the water, call down blessings on those who instruct people in beneficial knowledge."' (Tirmidhī)

'We, the Companions of Allah's Messenger ﷺ never asked 'Ā'ishah ﷺ about a tradition regarding which we were in doubt without finding that she had some knowledge of it.' (Tirmidhī)

Du'ā's Seeking Wisdom, Knowledge and Guidance

These *du'ā's* set the priorities for gaining knowledge. They show us that whatever we pursue, whatever skill or field of learning, it is never in isolation. Our knowledge, our directions, our time, and how these impact our souls, are all woven together. *Du'ā's* seeking knowledge are entwined with the qualities of courage, humility and strengthening our *īmān*.

O My Sustainer! Bestow wisdom on me and join me with the righteous. Grant me honourable mention on the tongues of truth among the later generation, and make me one of the inheritors of the garden of Bliss. (Surah *al-Shu'arā'* 26:83–85)

Supplication of the Prophet Nūḥ, ﷺ
Nūḥ said: 'O my Sustainer! I seek refuge with You, from asking You for that of which I have no knowledge. And unless You forgive me and have mercy on me, I should indeed be among the losers.' (Surah *Hūd* 11:47)

Supplication of the Prophet Mūsā, ﷺ
Mūsā said: 'O my Sustainer! Open my breast for me; and ease my task for me, and remove the impediment from my speech, so they may understand what I say.'
(Surah *Tā Hā* 20:25-28)

Those sustaining the throne [of Allah], and those around it celebrating the praises of their Sustainer, believing in Him and imploring forgiveness for those who believe, [pray]: ' Our Sustainer! You embrace all things in mercy and knowledge. Forgive, then, those who turn to You in repentance and follow

Your way, and preserve them from the chastisement of the
blazing Fire. And cause them, Our Sustainer, to enter the
Gardens of eternity that You have promised them.'
(Surah *al-Mu'min* 40:7–8)

'When the Messenger of Allah ﷺ awoke at night, he said:
"There is no god but You. Glory be to You,
O Allah. I ask Your pardon for my sin and I ask You for Your
mercy. O Allah! Advance me in knowledge. Do not cause
my heart to deviate (from guidance) after You have guided
me, and grant me mercy from Yourself for indeed You are the
Bestower of all grace."' (Abū Dāwūd)

'The Prophet ﷺ used to say after the dawn Prayer:
"O Allah, I ask You for knowledge that is beneficial,
deeds that are acceptable to You, and sustenance that
is wholesome."' (Muslim)

'O Allah I seek Your protection from misguiding others
or being misguided; from erring or others causing me
to err; from oppressing others or being oppressed;
and from acting ignorantly or others acting ignorantly
towards me.' (Abū Dāwūd)

'O my Sustainer, help me in remembering You, in being
grateful to You and in worshipping You in an excellent
manner.' (Abū Dāwūd)

Renowned for Her Intelligence, Illustrious in Her Knowledge

ʿĀʾishah al-Ṣiddīqah ﷺ**: The one who affirms the truth
Wife of the Noble Prophet** ﷺ

A lifetime of scholarship and learning started at a young age for ʿĀʾishah ﷺ, wife of the Prophet ﷺ and also the 'Mother of Believers'. Born to believing parents who were themselves learned, she inherited a thirst for knowledge early on. Abū Bakr ﷺ, her father, was a literary man and an expert in the science of genealogy. He was also a prominent businessman.

The lady ʿĀʾishah's married life was lived entirely in Madinah, where she grew and matured in tandem with the community of believers. Her sharp mind was very receptive to learning and understanding, and her excellent memory facilitated her memorizing the Qurʾan, famous poetry and eloquent speech, in addition to her extensive memory of medicinal remedies.

But this was only where her scholarship began. She fully understood the Qurʾanic sciences and specifically instructed in the application of the laws of inheritance, which involves precise mathematical calculations.

What she gained in the close company of the Prophet ﷺ was by no means kept to herself, for ʿĀʾishah ﷺ was renowned for conducting classes for male and female students, some of whom would travel far to join her teaching sessions. It was said, by one Companion, ʿUrwah ibn al-Zubayr: 'I did not see a greater scholar than ʿĀʾishah in the learning of the Qurʾan, shares of inheritance, lawful and unlawful matters, poetry and

literature, Arab history and genealogy,' and Abū Mūsā
al-Ashʿarī said: 'Whenever we, the Companions of the
Prophet ﷺ, encountered any difficulty in the matter of any
hadith, we referred it to ʿĀʾishah ؓ and found that she had
definite knowledge about it.'

In the half a century she lived after the death of the Prophet ﷺ
she shared many details of his private and public life by way of
teaching others his Divinely-inspired conduct and behaviour.
Thus she transmitted over 2,200 *aḥādīth*. Her position in
Madinah was incontestably superior to any other woman in
reaching intellectual heights, although many others trod the
path of learning after her and during her lifetime, contributing
to the body of knowledge that exists until this day.

Her public involvement, like that of her female contemporaries,
had much to do with alleviating the suffering and fulfilling
the needs of the disadvantaged. To this end, she distributed
whatever came her way, be it food, money, clothes or gifts she
received. During the Caliphate of ʿUmar ؓ, the treasury grew
from the collection of taxes. Concerned that the money should
reach the right people, a register of the elderly in Madinah
was drawn up and the distribution of funds was managed
by ʿĀʾishah ؓ.

Through her own transmission and admission, we have
inherited an honest and earthly view of this noble lady's home
life. We read of her strengths and weaknesses, her personal
limitations, as well as her spiritual vigour whereby she would
stand the long hours of the night in prayer with the Prophet
of God, peace be upon them both. Like each and every person
who walks this earth, ʿĀʾishah, ؓ was destined to have a
particular role – hers was that of scholarship and as a devoted

wife to the Prophet . She was fully aware of the privilege of being the wife of God's last Prophet to humankind. It was not her role to be a 'mother' in the conventional sense, but her position as the Prophet's wife accorded her the title of 'Mother of the Believers', and this she accomplished by educating the minds of the Muslims, during her lifetime and for centuries beyond.

The Heart
Seas of
Change

Without doubt, in the remembrance of God, hearts do find satisfaction. (Surah *al-Ra'd* 13:28)

The Heart

The condition of our *qalb* and *fu'ād* or heart – that part of us that thinks and feels, that guides our minds and 'sees' – is central to our lives. It turns through countless axes, revolving, coiling and uncoiling, rotating between peace and turmoil, light and darkness and all that lies between.

Our heart, the core of our being, is not left unguided. God, the Most Wise and the Source of Peace, has given us guidance and inspiration for keeping our hearts in the best condition. Rasūlu'llāh ﷺ had a soft heart; tender enough to stop his Companions from playing with fledgling birds, gentle-hearted enough to comfort a distressed tree next to his *minbar* in the *masjid*.

In our early years our hearts were naturally pure, not bearing grudges, spontaneous and honest. As time goes on, the tests upon the heart come from all directions, as our emotions and mind travel to new places. Our hearts will go through turmoil just as the hearts of the Prophets were tested. Their hearts were connected to those they loved too; they felt sorrow, grief, loneliness and regret. Their hearts cried out to their Lord as ours do and were guided by the All Merciful when the strength of emotions overtook them. Their hearts longed for companionship, security and safety. And their hearts hurt for their children, too.

A father and Prophet, Nūḥ ﷺ called out to Allah *subḥānahu wa ta'ālā* about his son, fearing he would drown with those who turned away from his message. Prophet Nūḥ ﷺ was reminded not to ask for things he knows nothing about, hence he immediately corrected himself with the supplication: '*My Lord, I take refuge with You from asking for things I know nothing about. If You do not forgive me, and have mercy on me, I shall be one of the losers.*'

The tests on the Prophets' hearts give us a glimpse of what they underwent, and the many storms they survived with integrity teach us in countless ways.

Certainty in God's decree springs from a well-kept heart. There is then no fear, and there is the reassurance that nothing in the heavens or the earth can take place without His command – He is *'Allām al-Ghuyūb*, the Knower of the Unseen. If the heart is left without this consciousness and without this care, it becomes hard, unable to cope with the demands of loss, pain and suffering.

You know and understand your heart better than anyone else does, except for *al-Khabīr*, the All Aware. Drawing closer to our Creator through remembrance (*dhikr*), seeking forgiveness, supplicating (making *duʿāʾs*) and praising the Prophet Muhammad ﷺ, are all channels to keeping our hearts alive.

Our hearts, like the great seas of this planet, are home to many scenes. Sometimes storm-like, when waves rage, blinding and deafening, we see no way out. *Ṣabr,* or forbearance and perseverance, brings a new scene the next day and the same sea radiates a sense of harmony as it cradles its waters, inviting warmth from above, sustaining life beneath.

Myriad Voices

'On my journey I tread life's path of tests and trials.
Tests of pain and pleasure, success and failure,
Trials of fear and hope.
Hopeful am I of walking in the shade of His Mercy,
Stepping in the light of His Guidance,
The Praiseworthy, The Giver of Peace.'

'Faces appear and speak a foreign tongue; some words I've
heard before, in some distant past, yet now I don't understand.
One after the other they come before me, some with eyes dry,
other with tears, they repeat some words… "We understand…
we are sorry. How? Are? You?"
I do not understand. All I know is the numbness that
overcame me with the loss. The emptiness that has filled me
with the questions of how I will carry on, how will life carry
on? Will light ever come to interrupt the feeling of utter
darkness all around me?'

'I had never been to sea, but when I drifted away from true
faith, I experienced drowning. I learnt what it felt like to lose
all sense of hope when the currents pulled me down further
and further. I lost all strength to search for a handhold, for
some way to survive. I lost all hope and was resigned that
when the waters are so deep, they silently consume you and
you are lost as though you never were once alive. Calling out
was my last and only attempt. Calling out to the Owner of my

soul, to the Self-sufficient, in need of nothing and no one.
The answer came to my call, and I lived again.'

'This heart: It resides somewhere outside time
Out there between the mountain echoes and
the myna's chirp…
It sides, sliding this way, then that
It hides, behind masks and masquerades in cloaks
It confides, whispering to the soul of moon-washed waters and
star-filled fields above
Lost and found
Contained and liberated
Where is it
This heart?'

'Just when your heart thought it was home and dry, safe in
the comfort of familiarity, of recognizing the inlets and bays,
of knowing when the tide comes in and out, it's faced with
a monstrous current, an unrecognizable beast, dislodging it,
disorientating it.
Just when it learnt the rules of navigating the dips and rises,
the rocks and basins, scaling the heights, this current carries it
to a new world. Sink again, flaying arms, strive again, plunge
again, come up for air and rise again, swim again until you
make these new waters your home.'

Dawn breaks in nameless shades
Lightening, glowing, spilling out.
Orange, red and yellow run into each other
Pots of colour dribble out and flood the sky.
Soaking the background, igniting the trees,
enveloping the mountains.
Where darkness filled their leaves and branches, there now
Dawn breaks and fills each vein with its light.

Have faith.
Hold through the night.
Dawn breaks and fills the void
Like some force, some megalith force,
Pushing away the black,
Taking its place and standing where blinding darkness veiled
all life.

A fern-grey mist passes by and clouds out the new sight,
Takes the light away – for a while.
Yet falling and lingering on the way,
That too moves on,
And,
Dawn breaks bringing with it a new day.

'Sometimes there are no words.
There are colours; unnamed hues and shades.
There are sounds; the vibes of tone, pitch and timing.
There are textures; grainy, marble cool, wooden warm.
Letters are locked in their names and words become prisoners.
This time, for the heart's liberty, there are no words.'

The Eternal Sources

Tests and hardships are a part of every life. The promise for this is from our Sustainer, *al-Fattāh* – the Reliever. We can encounter tests in innumerable ways – through health, wealth, possessions or relationships.

Or do you think that you shall enter Paradise without such [trials] as came to those who passed away before you? They encountered suffering and adversity, and were so shaken in spirit that even the Messenger and those of faith who were with him cried: 'When [will come] the help of Allah?' Ah! Certainly, the help of Allah is [always] near. (Surah *al-Baqarah* 2:114)

How many of the Prophets fought [in God's way], and with them [fought] large companies of devout people? But they never lost heart if they met with disaster in Allah's way, nor did they weaken [in will] nor give in. And God loves those who are firm and steadfast. (Surah *Āl 'Imrān* 3:146)

And We shall try you until We test those among you who strive their utmost and persevere in patience; and We shall try your reported [mettle]. (Surah *Muhammad* 47:31)

If God were to enlarge the provision of His servants, they would indeed transgress beyond all bounds, throughout the earth. But He sends down in due measure whatever [sustenance] He wills. (Surah *al-Shūrā* 42:27)

No misfortune can happen on earth or in your souls but is recorded in a Decree before We bring it into existence: That is truly easy for God. [This is] so that you may not despair over matters that pass you by, nor exult over favours bestowed upon

you, for God does not love any vainglorious boaster.
(Surah *al-Ḥadīd* 57:22–23)

'Narrated Abū Hurayrah: "Allah's Messenger ﷺ said, 'If any one of you looked at a person who was made superior to him in property and in worldly rank and in (good) appearance, then he should also look at the one who is inferior to him'."'
(Ibn Abī al-Dunyā)

'God's Messenger ﷺ said, Allah says: "I have nothing to give but Paradise as a reward to My servant, a true believer of Islam who, if I cause his dear friend (or relative) to die, remains patient (and hopes for Allah's reward)."' (*Ḥadīth Qudsī*)

Yet our tests and trials are not alone; they come with the promise of ease with hardship. When we turn to God, *Khayr-n-Nasirin*, the Best of Helpers, we are assured of this help and need to have hope.

So, truly with every difficulty, there is relief.
Truly with every difficulty there is relief.
Therefore, when you are free from [your immediate task] still labour hard in devotion, and turn [all] your attention to your Sustainer. (Surah *Alam Nashraḥ* 94:5–8)

Indeed, for the friends of God there is no fear, nor shall they grieve – those who believe and guard [constantly] against evil. For them are glad tidings, in the life of the present and in the Hereafter.

No change can there be in the words of Allah. This is indeed the supreme triumph. (Surah *Yūnus*, 10:62–64)

God desires ease for you, He does not desire hardship for you...
(Surah *al-Baqarah* 2:185)

Whosoever has consciousness of God, He will make matters easy for him. (Surah *al-Ṭalāq* 65:4)

As for the one who believes and acts rightly, he will receive the best of rewards and we will issue a command making things easy for him. (Surah *al-Kahf* 18:88)

Let the person of means spend according to his means: and the person whose resources are restricted, let him spend according to what God has given him. God puts no burden on any person beyond what He has given him. After a difficulty, God will soon grant relief. (Surah *al-Ṭalāq* 65:7)

'The Messenger of Allah ﷺ said, "Temptations are presented to the heart, one by one. Any heart that accepts them will be left with a black stain, but any heart that rejects them will be left with a mark of purity, so that hearts are of two types: a dark heart that has turned away and become like an overturned vessel, and a pure heart that will never be harmed by temptation for as long as the earth and the heavens exist. The dark heart only recognises good and denounces evil when this suits its desires and whims."' (Muslim)

'Remarkable are the ways of a believer for there is good in every affair of his, for this is not the case with others except the believer. If he has an occasion to feel delight, he thanks (God), thus there is a good for him in it; and if he finds himself in difficulty and submits (and endures it patiently), there is a good for him in it.' (Muslim)

'In Paradise there are pillars of rubies on which there are rooms of emeralds with open doors shining like a star. He was asked "Who will occupy them?" He replied,
"Those who love one another for God's sake, those who sit together for God's sake and those who visit one another for God's sake."' (Al-Bazzār)

Sometimes when we are overwhelmed by anxiety and unease, this is often the result of our own actions. How easily do we shift the cause elsewhere; to a person, a place, a situation? In reality, when we have wronged our souls our hearts feel discontent and unrest, hence we meet distress. Reflecting on this brings deeper self-awareness and deals with the seed of our unrest.

If anyone does evil or wrongs his own soul but afterwards seeks forgiveness he will find God All Forgiving, Most Merciful.
If anyone earns a sin, he earns it against his own soul, for God is All Knowing, All Compassionate. (Surah *al-Nisā'*, 4:110–111)

Those who, having committed an act of indecency to be ashamed of, or have wronged their own souls, remember Allah and ask for forgiveness for their sins – and who can forgive sins except Allah? – and do not wilfully persist in [the wrong] they have committed. They shall be recompensed by forgiveness from their Sustainer. (Surah *Āl 'Imrān* 3:135–136)

But no sooner does He deliver them, behold, they transgress insolently on the earth in defiance of right! O mankind! Your insolence is against your own souls. Enjoy the life of the present;

in the end to Us is your return, and then We shall show you the truth of all that you did. (Surah *Yūnus* 10:23)

And who does more wrong than one who is reminded of the signs of his Sustainer, but turns away from them, forgetting the [deeds] which his hands have sent forth? Indeed, We have set veils over their hearts so that they understand this not, and over their ears We have caused deafness. If you call them to the Right Path, even then will they never accept guidance. (Surah *al-Kahf* 18:57)

Whatever pain we go through, whether it is from others or through our own doing, the forgiveness and mercy from God – *al-'Afūw*, the Ever Pardoning, *al-Ghaffār*, the Ever Forgiving – brings hope without measure. It is for us to seek with sincerity and maintain the will to refrain from the same mistakes.

Say: 'O My servants who have transgressed against their souls. Despair not of the mercy of God, for God forgives all sins.' (Surah *al-Zumar*, 39:53)

And whoever does evil or wrongs himself but afterwards seeks Allah's forgiveness, he will find Allah All Forgiving, Most Merciful. (Surah *al-Nisā'* 4:110)

O you who have attained to faith, remain conscious of God and believe in His Messenger, and He will grant you doubly of His grace, and will light for you a light wherein you shall walk, and will forgive you [your past sins], for God is Most Forgiving, a dispenser of Grace. (Surah *al-Ḥadīd* 57:28)

Your Sustainer knows best what is in your hearts: If you do deeds of righteousness, indeed He is Most Forgiving to those who turn to Him again and again [in true penitence].
(Surah *Banī Isrāʾīl* 17:25)

And O my People! Ask forgiveness of your Sustainer, and turn to Him [in repentance]. He will pour abundant rain on you from the skies, and add strength to your strength. So do not turn back in sin! (Surah *Hūd* 11:52)

There are countless calls that beckon us with hollow promises of peace: distractions that can lull the senses for a while. Ultimately, there is one place, we are assured, we will find peace and comfort for our hearts: in the remembrance of God – *al- Raḥmān*, the Compassionate, *al-Wadūd*, the Loving.

Has not the time arrived for the believers that their hearts in all humility should engage in the remembrance of Allah and of the Truth which has been revealed [to them], and that they should not become like those to whom was given Revelation before, and then a long time passed and their hearts grew hard? For many among them are now depraved. (Surah *al-Ḥadīd* 57:16)

The true believers are those who, when Allah is mentioned, feel a tremor in their hearts, and when they hear His revelations recited, find their faith strengthened, and they put [all] their trust in their Sustainer. (Surah *al-Anfāl* 8:2)

O mankind! There has come to you an admonition from your Sustainer and a healing for the [diseases] in your hearts. And for

those who believe, a guidance and a mercy. (Surah *Yūnus* 10:57)
And should you forget, remember your Sustainer...
(Surah *al-Kahf* 18:24)

*Those who believe and whose hearts find rest in the remembrance
of God. Certainly, in the remembrance of God do hearts find
rest. For those who believe and act righteously is [every] blessedness,
and a beautiful place of [final] return.* (Surah *al-Raʿd* 13:28–29)

*And We send down from the Qurʾan that which is a healing and
a mercy to those who believe.* (Surah *Banī Isrāʾīl* 17:82)

*Is one whose heart God has opened to Islam, so that he has
received enlightenment from Allah [be no better than one
hard-hearted]?*
*Woe to those whose hearts are hardened against celebrating the
praises of God. They are manifestly wandering [in error]!*
*Allah has revealed [from time to time] the most beautiful Message
in the form of a Book, consistent with itself, [yet] repeating [its
teaching in various aspects]. The skins of those who fear their
Sustainer tremble; then their skins and their hearts soften to the
celebration of Allah's praises. Such is the guidance of Allah. He
guides whom He pleases, but those Allah leaves to stray can have
none to guide them.* (Surah *al-Zumar* 39:22–23)

'Keep your tongue moist with the remembrance of Allah.'
(Tirmidhī)

'Ibn Ḥajar ﷺ said: "When he spoke of remembering Allah
(*dhikr*), he meant doing it regularly and persistently, by doing
acts that are obligatory or encouraged, such as reciting the
Qurʾan, reading hadith, and studying with other people."'
(*Fatḥ al-Bārī*, 11/209)

Tranquillity envelops a heart that trusts solely in the decree of God – *al-Ḥāfiẓ*, the Protector, *al-Rāfiʿ*, the One Who Elevates (in rank).

No calamity occurs without the permission of God; and whoever trusts in God, He guides his heart along the Right Path; and God knows all things. (Surah *al-Taghābun* 64:11)

If Allah helps you, none can overcome you, and if He forsakes you, who is there after Him that can help you? It is in Allah alone that believers put their trust. (Surah *Āl ʿImrān* 3:160)

So do not weaken, nor fall into despair. For you must surely gain mastery if you are true in faith. (Surah *Āl ʿImrān* 3:139)

'The Messenger of Allah ﷺ said: "The hearts of the children of Adam are as one between the fingers of the Most Merciful, and He turns them in whatever way He wills." Then he said: "O Allah, Controller of the hearts, direct our hearts to obey You."' (Muslim)

Du'ā's on Turning Our Hearts

These *du'ā's* are a balm – the healing, the succour no person can offer. They beseech the Almighty – the Owner of our hearts for faith, strength, and resolution. They seek protection and courage and guide us to higher ideals of forgiveness and repairing ties which can easily be forgotten at times of stress. The reminder to pray for others, as well as for oneself is itself therapeutic as it elevates the heart to another level of consciousness and gratitude.

'O Allah, I seek refuge in Thee from incapacity and laziness, from cowardice and miserliness, from decrepitude and from the torment of the grave.

O Allah, grant to my soul the sense of righteousness and purify it, for You are the Best Purifier thereof. You are the Protecting friend thereof, and the Guardian thereof.

O Allah, I seek refuge in You from the knowledge which does not benefit, from the heart that has no fear (of Allah), from the soul that is not contented and from the supplication that is not responded to.' (Muslim)

'Our Sustainer! Let not our hearts deviate now after You have guided us, but grant us mercy from You; for You are the Grantor of bounties without measure.' (Surah Āl 'Imrān 3:8)

'Our Sustainer! Forgive us, and our brethren who came before us into the Faith, and leave not in our hearts any rancour [or sense of injury] against those who have believed. Our Sustainer! You are indeed Full of Kindness, Most Merciful.' (Surah al-Ḥashr 59:10)

'Our Sustainer! We have wronged our own souls: If You do not forgive us and bestow Your Mercy upon us, we shall certainly be among the losers.' (Surah *al-A'rāf* 7:23)

'My Lord, I am truly in great need of any good that You might send down to me.' (Surah *al-Qaṣaṣ* 28:24)

'O Allah, Guide me with those whom You have guided, and strengthen me with those whom You have given strength, and take me to Your care with those whom You have taken to Your care, and bless me in what You have given me.' (Abū Dāwūd)

'O Allah! You are my Sustainer, there is no deity but You. You Created me and I am Your servant and I am trying my best to keep my Oath (of faith) to You and to seek to live in the hope of Your Promise.

I seek Refuge in You from my greatest evil deeds. I acknowledge Your Blessings upon me and my sins. So forgive me, for none but You can forgive sins.' (Bukhārī)

Unfaltering in Her Faith, Courageous in Her Endurance

Āsiyah ⬥: Believer and wife of the Pharaoh

Centuries ago, the Nile witnessed one of the most renowned episodes in its rich history, the chapter of its carrying a Prophet of God, whilst its banks were home to one of the world's worst, most notorious tyrants – the Pharaoh.

It was by its bank, as dusk unravelled its lustrous threads over the river, that a basket carrying the baby Mūsā ⬥, was pushed by the waves towards the shore. A maiden, seeing the basket bob up to the reeds, made a clearing and reached out, hoisting the basket up and out of the river.

Laden with the weight of the basket, she hurried back to the Pharaoh's palace where she served and placed it before none other than the Pharaoh's gracious wife, Āsiyah ⬥. When Āsiyah ⬥ lifted the cover, her eyes fell on the delightful sight of an endearing baby boy, alive and well. Āsiyah ⬥ was of a compassionate nature, and she embraced the baby as soon as she set eyes on him. His tiny body rested on hers as she held him tight. On seeing her attraction to the child, the heartless Pharaoh ordered he should be killed or given away. After all, he who thought he was god could exercise his command over every life, especially when he perceived the baby boy as a threat to his kingdom.

Āsiyah 🌸 spoke out against the brutal command of her husband, and insisted on keeping the child, pleading that he may be 'a delight to my eye and yours'. Thus, she became the adoptive mother of the baby Mūsā 🌸.

By God's mercy, Mūsā's real mother, unknown to the rest of the palace, was employed to suckle her baby after he had refused a succession of suckling foster-mothers that preceded her. It was only a little earlier that she had been inspired by God to set the baby afloat on the Nile; for the river would take him to his destiny. Although this was difficult for her, she did it, trusting in God, for He strengthened her heart with faith.

Thus did we return Mūsā to his mother
that her eyes may be delighted
and she is not grieved,
and that she would know
that the promise of Allah is true. (Surah *al-Qaṣaṣ* 28:13)

With the passage of time, the signs of Mūsā's Propethood became more evident. Those whose hearts were willing to see, saw the powers with which God had endowed him and submitted their selves in belief. Āsiyah 🌸 was also one of the believers. Although she saw how others in the Pharaoh's court had been killed for their belief, how her maid was tortured for her belief, how she stood to lose all the luxuries that surrounded her, she remained an unswerving believer, in spite of her husband's rage and wrath.

Being the wife of Pharaoh did not spare her from the torture he inflicted on those who believed in Mūsā's message to surrender to the One God of the earth, sky and the universe – Allah. Instead, she had much pain meted out to her.

Her spirit was strong and she bore with firmness what came her way, trusting in the help of her Sustainer. Yet, finally when her body could take no more of Pharaoh's trials on her, she prayed with her dying breath:

'O my Sustainer! Build for me,
in nearness to You, a house in Paradise,
and save me from Pharaoh and his doings,
and save me from those that do wrong.'
(Surah *al-Taḥrīm* 66:11)

Her soul departed from this world, destined for the highest ranks in Paradise. Whilst many pharaohs and nobles tried to immortalize themselves by the banks of the Nile, Āsiyah's strength and struggle lives on in the hearts of believers.

Health and Appearance
Lakes and Reflections

He created the heavens and earth for a true purpose;
He formed you and made your forms good: you will all
return to Him. (Surah *al-Taghābun* 64:3)

Health and Appearance

The human form, shaped by the Fashioner, is the vessel, the container of your mind, heart, soul and spirit. A carriage which takes its direction from inside. Your body is precious; it is a manifestation of your inner self. Your countenance is the creation of God – *al-Musawwir*, the Bestower of Forms, *al-Muqīt*, the Powerful. It is He Who has created your unique disposition. From the time you occupy your given place on earth, your body is placed in your care.

To lead a balanced life, we are obliged to fulfil our emotional, spiritual and mental needs as well as pay attention to our body's wellbeing. When we have good physical health, it's a huge blessing that enables us to be productive and facilitates our spiritual growth. In reality though, we live in a time of imbalances; there is either an obsession with one's physical health to the exclusion of their spiritual wellness; or spiritual needs are addressed at the cost of physical health. These contradictions within ourselves need to be addressed first, if we want to sustain holistic wellbeing. Taking the Qur'anic perspective and tradition of the Prophets ﷺ, these areas of our health are not separated, but entwined when our wellbeing, faith and destiny in the Hereafter are the subject. *Āyahs* (verses, signs) about our thoughts, feelings, actions and the best outcome for a person illustrate these connections time and again, as one finds when they travel through the sacred sources.

The blessings of good mental and physical health are countless; ask one who cannot walk about the gift of mobility; ask one who cannot swallow about the miracle of the muscles in our throat, which we use without thinking all our lives; ask one struggling with fears or trauma about the freedom of having a tranquil, settled mind. There are endless struggles people have with their health in the widest sense.

Respecting our appearance is equally significant. Surrounding us are constant reminders of how society blurs the lines about respecting a woman's body and exploiting it; how often does commerce rely on the woman's body, and who is it that gives permission for its use? In contrast, the sacred sources reinforce respecting and caring about one's appearance. Anything which is precious is kept wisely. It is nurtured but not worshiped, adorned but not flaunted.

The ever-changing definitions of 'beauty' need not trouble an informed mind, as natural beauty is not subject to continuous change. If we contemplate how lakes exist in all different forms – from deep Highland lochs to small mountain tarns – we can draw parallels to reflect on our own selves. Each of the world's lakes are different in their depth and environment, creating varied habitats for the life that grows from them. Yet each one is serene; its waters glisten, reflecting the beauty of its own distinct surroundings, unperturbed and inspiring.

Myriad Voices

'My form has been created by the Maker and the Fashioner. My body encases my soul, heart and mind; it is the vehicle to manifest obedience to my Sustainer. My body holds the blessings of so many faculties; a structure which no mind or hand on earth has yet been able to replicate.'

'Precious: I am the carriage that is home to new life, carrying the force that drives the human race forward. My joints and limbs may serve and help many, but my submission is only to the Creator and Sustainer of humankind.'

'How can I feel whole when I have been taught to care and invest only in my "body"? Society has severed my soul and heart from my limbs and so I merely exist in the outward form. To be complete I need to be reunited with my rightful partners; only then can I be alive to the demands of being an inheritor of God's earth.'

Health and Appearance

'Beneath my glowing appearance, carefully selected, accidentally casual look, lies my mind's tsunami; a stranger to me, an ever present shadow, an unwanted confidant that consumes days and weeks of my life. Within its vortex disappears my personality: I watch it vanish. I watch my self dissolve. I wait for my return.

In the meantime there are masks and costumes I masquerade
in. I maintain a character for the name I own, one that doesn't
betray the storm inside me.
Waiting for my return.
Waiting for my mind's wellbeing.
Waiting to set the façade aside and retrieve the days and weeks
as my life.'

'"Why enshroud it, why cover it, why deny you have a body?"
Said her pitiful look, as she watched me board the train.
"Yes, I have a body, I respect it, and it's the vessel of my mind
and spirit." Said my glance as a refrain.'

'The moment we met, my face evaporated, as did my words
and mind. They transpired like mist falling. All you saw in me
was the one square metre of material worn on my head.
Your hostile looks said it all.
That was all you saw, and the reflection on your face showed
your jolted thoughts that are not "polite" to say in public.
As I reminisced about our childhood games we played together,
you neither heard nor remembered. The one square metre
of material had grown in size and now covered our past, and
probably any future too.'

'Is my commitment to dress modestly the real cause of so much speculation? Or do people feel threatened by a mind that makes independent choices and voices a commitment to the One Cherisher and Sustainer, greater than my commitment to their fashion standards?'

The Eternal Sources

For our holistic wellbeing, it helps if we equip ourselves with a positive and grateful outlook. When we take the foundation of reliance on Allah *subḥānahu wa taʿālā*, trusting in Him and accepting His decree, we stand on balanced ground. At the same time, there may be times when we need to and should seek medical and professional help. These two ways of caring for our health are not in conflict, rather one complements the other.

It is reported in a hadith on the authority of ʿAbdullāh ibn ʿAbbās, who said: 'One day I was behind the Prophet ﷺ and he said to me: "Young man, I shall teach you some words [of advice]:

> Be mindful of Allah, and Allah will protect you. Be mindful of Allah, and you will find Him in front of you. If you ask, ask of Allah; if you seek help, seek help of Allah. Know that if the Nation were to gather together to benefit you with anything, it would benefit you only with something that Allah had already prescribed for you, and that if they gather together to harm you with anything, they would harm you only with something Allah had already prescribed for you. The pens have been lifted and the pages have dried."

Prophet Muhammad ﷺ said, "Look at those who are less fortunate than yourselves, not at those who are better off than yourselves, so that you will not belittle the blessings that Allah has bestowed upon you." (Bukhārī)

'And never give up hope of Allah's soothing Mercy: truly no one despairs of Allah's soothing Mercy except those who have no faith.'
(Surah *Yūsuf* 12:87)

And for those who fear Allah, He always prepares a way out, and He provides for him from sources he could never imagine. And if anyone puts his trust in Allah, sufficient is Allah for him. For Allah will surely accomplish His purpose; verily, for all things has Allah appointed a due proportion. (Surah *al-Ṭalāq* 65:2–3)

The body is a trust from God, *al-Jalīl*, the Glorious and Exalted. It is a sign of His Magnificence; its intricacies and countless abilities are a demonstration of the Creator's craft. This cherished gift is our vehicle in this life.

'Our Sustainer! You have not created all this without a purpose.'
(Surah *Āl 'Imrān* 3:191)

'Fast as well as eat and drink. Stand in prayer, as well as sleep. Your body has a right over you and your eyes have a right over you…' said the noble Prophet ﷺ. (Bukhārī)

'The Prophet ﷺ said, "There are two blessings which many people lose: (They are) health and free time for doing good."' (Muslim)

'The Prophet ﷺ said: "A physically able believer is better than a weak believer."' (Muslim)

To look after our bodies is an act of worship. Caring for its health starts by nourishing our bodies with what is pure and wholesome, in moderation. The earth gives us what is pure in abundance and this is blessed when it is shared. The world has the resources to feed each person with what is 'good and pure', but alas it is us, the inheritors of this earth who fail to distribute it equitably.

O believers! Eat of what is good and pure that We have provided for you and be grateful to Allah, if you truly worship Him. (Surah *al-Baqarah* 2:172)

O people! Eat of what is lawful and good on the earth and do not follow the footsteps of Satan, for he is your open enemy. (Surah *al-Baqarah* 2:168)

Eat and drink, but waste not in extravagance. Certainly, Allah likes not those who waste in extravagance. (Surah *al-Aʿrāf* 7:31)

'Eat of the good things We have provided for your sustenance, but commit no excess therein, lest My wrath should justly descend on you'. (Surah *Tā Hā* 20:81)

'The Prophet ﷺ said: "The worst vessel that the son of Adam can fill is his stomach." And he also said: "It is enough for the son of Adam to have just morsels (of food) to keep his back upright. But if you have to eat more than that then one-third for food, one-third for water, and one-third for air."' (Tirmidhī)

113

Health and Appearance

'The food of one person will be sufficient for two, and the food of two people will be sufficient for four, and the food of four will be sufficient for eight'. (Muslim)

For our enjoyment and wellbeing, we have been provided with countless kinds of sustenance of every texture, colour and flavour. Our sustenance is from God, _al-Akram_, the Most Bounteous, and we are reminded to have moderation in what we consume.

It is He who sends down rain from the sky; and with it We bring forth vegetation of all kinds, and out of it We bring forth thick clustered grain. And out of the date palm and its spate come clusters of dates hanging low and near, and gardens of grapes, olives and pomegranates each similar [in kind] yet different [in variety and taste]. Look at their fruits when they begin to bear, and the ripeness thereof. (Surah *al-An'ām* 6:99)

And behold from the fruits of the date palm and grapes you get wholesome drink and nutrition: Behold in this is a sign for those who are wise. (Surah *al-Nahl* 16:67)

And He it is Who produces gardens [of vine] – trellised and untrellised – and palms and seed-produce of which the fruits are of various sorts, and olives and pomegranates, like and unlike; eat of its fruit when it bears fruit, and pay His due on the day of its reaping, and do not act extravagantly; surely, He does not love the extravagant. (Surah *al-An'ām* 6:141)

And He has set the earth for all living creatures. Therein are fruit and palms with sheathed clusters of dates, and grain with [its] husk and fragrance. Which of the bounties of your Sustainer will you deny? (Surah *al-Raḥmān* 55:10–13)

Say: 'Who has forbidden the beautiful [gifts] of Allah, which He has produced for His servants, and the things, clean and pure, [which He has provided] for sustenance?' Say: 'They are, in the life of this world, for those who believe, [and] purely for them on the Day of Judgement.' Thus do We explain the signs in detail for those who understand. (Surah *al-Aʿrāf* 7:32)

O you who believe! Fasting is prescribed for you as it was prescribed for those before you, that you may learn self-restraint or taqwā. (Surah *al-Baqarah* 2:183)

'Whoever awakes in the morning with a healthy body, and a self that is sound, and whose provision is assured, he is like one who possesses the whole world.' (Tirmidhī)

''Ā'ishah, the Mother of the Faithful, narrated that she was on a journey along with the Apostle of Allah ﷺ: "I had a race with him (the Prophet ﷺ) and I won. When I became fleshy, I had (another) race with him and he won. He said: 'We are now even'."' (Abū Dāwūd)

'The Prophet ﷺ said: "Allah has sent down both the disease and the cure, and He has appointed a cure for every disease, so treat yourselves medically, but use nothing unlawful."' (Abū Dāwūd)

And Who, when I am sick, restores me to health. (Surah *al-Shuʿarā* 26:80)

'Be moderate, and you will reach what you want.' (Bukhārī)

When we value our bodies, we respect them and raise them above the public gaze to the sanctuary of *ḥayā* – a natural state of modesty and humility for men and women. What we wear and how we cover is then an extension of the heart's willingness to be close to God. The discussions, criticisms and dissecting of 'hijab' seem to forget that it is a soulful, faithful act of submission to *al-Shakūr*, the Rewarder of Good, in the same way keeping promises, fasting, or pilgrimage are acts of worship.

Modesty, or *ḥayā* that comes from *īmān*, is not a barrier for the covered person; the only veils that are a problem are the ones over the hearts of the criticisers.

He created the heavens and earth for a true purpose; He formed you and made your forms good: you will all return to Him. (Surah *al-Taghābun* 64:3)

O Prophet, tell your wives and daughters and the believing women to draw their outer garments around them [when they go out or are among men]. It is better so that they may be known [to be Muslims] and not annoyed. (Surah *al-Aḥzāb* 33:59)

Say to the believing men that they should lower their gaze and guard their modesty; that will make for greater purity for them, and Allah is well acquainted with all that they do.
And say to the believing women that they should lower their gaze and guard their modesty, and that they should not display their beauty and ornaments except what must ordinarily appear thereof; that they should draw their veils over their bosoms and not display their beauty except to their husbands.
(Surah *al-Nūr* 24:30–31)

O children of Adam! Wear your most beautiful apparel at every time and place of prayer; eat and drink, but waste not by excess, for Allah loves not the wasters. (Surah *al-Aʿrāf* 7:31)

'When you meet one another, neaten your clothes… so that you are a mark of beauty among people.' (*Sunan*, Abū Dāwūd)

'*Ḥayā* (modesty and humility) and *īmān* (faith in God) are fully joined together. If one is lost the other goes as well.' (*Al-Mustadrak*, al-Ḥākim)
'*Ḥayā* (modesty & humility) is from *īmān* (belief) and *īmān* is in Jannah (Paradise).' (Tirmidhī)

'ʿĀʾishah ﷺ reported that Asmāʾ ﷺ, the daughter of Abū Bakr ﷺ, (her sister) came to the Messenger of Allah ﷺ while wearing thin clothing. He approached her and said: "O Asmāʾ! When a girl reaches the menstrual age, it is not proper that anything should remain exposed except this and this." And he pointed to the face and hands.' (Abū Dāwūd)

'Whoever refrains from dressing (in fancy, expensive clothes) out of humility towards Allah, even though he is able to do so, Allah will call him on the Day of Resurrection at the head of His creation and will give him the choice of whatever garment of faith he wishes to wear.' (Tirmidhī)

'The Messenger of Allah ﷺ, said: "Your Lord is modest and generous and would never turn the hands of someone without gain when he raises them to Him (in supplication)."' (Tirmidhī and Abū Dāwūd)

Du'ā's for Our Wellbeing

These *du'ā*'s articulate the connection between our health, faith, this life and the Hereafter. Good health is the most precious gift we can ask for, and if we are blessed with it, it is the cause for unending gratitude.

Focusing deeply with *khushu* (concentration, sincerity) on our *du'ā*'s is one of the ways we can help our emotional and mental wellbeing too. In general, *du'ā*'s bring our relationship alive with Our Sustainer; we call on His attributes in response to our reality. Recognizing our needs and verbalizing the help we need is part of self-awareness and this, in itself, is an empowering way to take care of ourselves.

Supplications are connected to all our actions. When we have something new to wear, asking for the blessing within it and praying for the benefit of it is in keeping with all the actions of a believer. Whether going out, sleeping or eating, starting daily functions with, 'in the name of Allah' retains a sense of God-consciousness throughout our day.

'The Prophet ﷺ said: "O 'Abbās, ask Allah for health in this world and in the next."' (Al-Bazzār)

'Ask Allah for forgiveness and health. After certainty of faith, nothing better is given to a person than good health.' (Al-Nasā'ī)

'O Allah, make me content with what you have provided me, send blessings for me therein, and place for me every absent thing with something better.' (Bukhārī)

Supplication said when wearing a new garment

'O Allah for You is all praise, You have clothed me with (this garment). I ask You for the good of it and for the good of which it was made. And I seek refuge with You from the evil of it, and the evil for which it was made.' (Abū Dāwūd)

'O Allah, place light in my heart, light in my tongue,
light in my hearing, light in my sight,
light behind me, light in front of me, light on my right,
light on my left, light above me and light below me;
place light in my sinew, in my flesh, in my blood, in my hair and in my skin;
place light in my soul and make light abundant for me;
make me light and grant me light.' (Muslim)

'O Allah, make me healthy in my body.
O Allah, preserve for me my hearing.
O Allah, preserve for me my sight.
There is none worthy of worship but You.
O Allah, I seek refuge in You from disbelief and poverty and I seek refuge in You from the punishment of the grave. There is none worthy of worship but You.' (Abū Dāwūd)

Through Perception and Wisdom, Belief and Humility

Bilqīs ﷺ, Queen of Saba'

Saba' was a land of grandeur, opulent buildings, waterways and gardens. In its bustling capital of Ma'ārib, nothing seemed to be lacking and nothing detracted from its splendour. From the canals outside the city, its high walls were visible to onlookers. Only the privileged, however, could enter the gates into the grand courtyard, to approach the towering columns of the palace. Once inside, the visitor could behold the ruler, seated on her rare, exquisite throne. This was Bilqīs, the Queen of Saba'.

Possessing sharp faculties of discernment and judgement, she was independent and at the height of her reign – enhanced by her physical health and beauty.

It was this sight that the renowned hoopoe bird perceived and flew back to communicate to its ruler – Sulaymān, ﷺ – a king and Prophet who reigned over a land some distance away from Saba'. His gifts from God were numerous: his sound judgement and knowledge, his ability to communicate with birds and animals and his strength to liberate lands and spread truth as his prophetic role demanded of him. The hoopoe told Sulaymān ﷺ of the riches and splendour of the lands he had seen and also of the ruler and subjects who worshipped the sun instead of the Creator of the sun.

It distressed Sulaymān ﷺ that there were people who, after receiving the bounties of God, had covered their hearts from the truth and were bowing to the sun. He wrote to the Queen of Saba' inviting her and her subjects to acknowledge and submit to the One True God.

When she received the letter, Bilqīs made no hasty judgement but summoned her courtiers and advisers and said: 'O chiefs! Here is delivered to me a letter worthy of respect. It is from Solomon, and is (as follows):

Bismillāh ir-Raḥmān ir-Raḥīm –
"In the name of Allah, Most Gracious, The Ever Merciful.
Rise not up against me, but come to me in submission [to the true Religion]." (Surah *al-Naml* 27:29–30)

Bilqīs wanted to avoid the possibility of hostility between the two kingdoms. As a response to Sulaymān's letter, she decided to send gifts – samples of her splendours – to this king, and await the outcome. It is possible that she felt that a worldly king would accept her gifts and that a true prophet of God would not.

Sulaymān ﷺ received Bilqīs's ambassadors but returned the gifts she had sent. She decided then, to visit Sulaymān ﷺ herself and set out for a long journey. When he learned of her visit, he commanded one of his forces to bring her throne to his palace, and this, 'in a twinkling of an eye', was done.

The time for the meeting between Sulaymān ﷺ and the Queen of Saba' had arrived. On reaching the palace, she was presented with the throne, and remarked that it looked similar to her own; no doubt, internally amazed at the power and ability of the wise king. Following this, Bilqīs was invited to enter the magnificent palace of her host. When she stepped inside, to her amazement it was as though she was stepping into water. Thus she raised her rich gown to pass through the water with some ease. Reality isn't always what we think we see. Bilqīs was not standing on water, as the Prophet informed her, but on slabs of crystal with water below:

'This is but a palace paved smooth with slabs of glass.'
(Surah *al-Naml* 27:44)

The experience of being deceived by appearance and reality moved the heart of Bilqīs to submitting to the One God. Until then, the Queen had been worshipping what was created and not the Creator. In that moment of true inner perception, where her riches and outward glories became secondary to her inner yearnings for truth, she uttered the following words:

'O my Lord! I have indeed wronged my soul:
I do [now] submit [in Islam], with Sulaymān, to the Sovereign
Sustainer of all creation.' (Surah *al-Naml* 27:44)

Marriage

Clouds
and Seas

They are your garments and you are their garments.
(Surah *al-Baqarah* 2:187)

Marriage

The union of hearts, minds and souls in the institution of marriage is the oldest 'contract' between two people on this earth. Their coming together, bringing with them families and communities, has been the axis around which societies thrive and grow.

This contract is made in the name of God – *al-Shahīd*, the Witness, and *al-Raqīb*, the Ever Watchful. It is so central to the wellbeing of the individual and society, it is strongly recommended as a Sunnah of the noble Prophet ﷺ. As a stage of life many people experience, it should be based around love and mercy and not be feared and avoided. Nor should it be treated with a blasé attitude.

Whilst this Sunnah is commendable, families and communities need to value and support those who don't or can't get married. For some, it's their personal choice and for others it may be their fate, that in spite of their efforts and desire to find a spouse, they remain single. Increasingly, some people are single having left an oppressive marriage. Whatever their situation, the worth of a person is not tied to their marital status.

For married couples, the rights and responsibilities that unfold with marriage can at times be so challenging that to fulfil these is equated with fulfilling half of your faith. Entering this partnership is thus an act of worship that brings you closer to God.

In essence, each partner's role is to bring and receive harmony in a stable unit. Each needs the time and energy to work towards his or her spiritual and devotional goals.

A healthy marriage is the fluid sharing of responsibilities, the sensitivity to one another's abilities and duties for a peaceful companionship. The responsibility of mutual cooperation and the daily 'work' of sustaining a healthy marriage rests on both the husband and wife's shoulders. As a woman, your mental, physical and emotional gifts are inimitable. They equip you for a specific role and dimension that you can bring to share a tranquil union.

No two marriages can be alike; this is counter-intuitive. When each and every individual in the world is unique, how can the union of two individuals be like any other? Yet regular comparison and sharing of the minutiae of married life causes stress because no one measure applies to the variety of couples. The personal qualities you bring to your marriage – mental, physical, emotional – are tailored for your specific role. What another woman brings to her marriage will be different, for a different type of union: both thriving partnerships, both entirely distinct.

Within marriage, each *zawj* or partner as the Qur'an calls them, will have their own rhythm of life; their own journey; their hearts will be challenged in the ways written for them. This partnership is a means of supporting each other's journey with empathy, not competition and rivalry. Over time, this journey will change shape; ease and difficulty, health and *rizq* – one's provision – will diminish and increase. Neither the drought nor the monsoon lasts forever.

A symbiotic relationship, marriage rests on the husband and wife working together to build the foundation on which society grows. Like the rain cycle: the clouds and the sea have an interdependent relationship. The unseen workings of the wind merge sea and clouds from which the rain appears. Together they work, relying on each other's roles, giving and receiving to keep the world's most essential cycle continuing.

Myriad Voices

'I enter this contract, this act of worship, in the name of Our Creator and Sustainer, as a servant of God. I enter this sacred institution to grow and enrich my life and that of others. My companion on this journey is one who fears God in all matters, and who knows his return is ultimately to God, the Sublime, the All-Forgiving.'

'My wedding list:
* need: spiritual, emotional, intellectual togetherness, respect and value;
* give: respect, thanks, encouragement, commitment, and space;
* share: prayers, time, interests, trips, sunrises and sunsets.'

'Some clothes just don't fit, won't fit. They checked and rechecked to see if it would fit me, and I, it. I was told repeatedly of its creation and its 'one of a kind' unique qualities.

The day came when I was to wear this garment. From the beginning, the weight of the fabric stifled me and pulled me down.

Too heavy from its oppressive load I couldn't walk, there was no room to move or grow. Soon, I was fighting to breathe.

This wasn't warmth, protection and beautifying. To the rest of the world it looked like this "garment" was exquisite, people sought out ones similar.

Only I knew the tyranny of its weave. This wasn't a "fit"; this wasn't a marriage I could wear any longer.'

'Looking back over half a century of married life is like taking a long look at a familiar garden. When an owner first tends to her or his new garden, so much planning and thought, sensitivity and creativity are spent. Colour, texture and scent, the artistry of nature is available to cultivate and enjoy.

Once the planting is completed, the seasons work their wonders and bring forth their finery to the eyes of the beholder. Each leaf and petal, blade of grass and stem bring joy to those who walk through it and enjoy the sight. Even when rain, winds and chill set in, the gardener continues to take care of these riches. The seasons pass again, and the next year, the colours are more vivid, the trees are stronger, their stems reaching further out to offer shade to passers-by.

Time adds maturity. Though the scene may vary from year to year, the changing tones and hues bring ever-increasing pleasure.

So too is the case with marriage. In the beginning one is conscientious, paying attention and having the time to listen, share, and care. Everyone around feels the beauty that emanates from a marriage that is cared for. Weeding is regularly done to inhibit the growth of the deep roots of future problems.

Yet, as the web of responsibilities grow, it becomes so easy to forget the landscape that was once so attentively planned. Husband and wife become fixtures, just part of the scenery, like the cedar tree that is just another tree now; no longer having a 'presence' the way it used to. Instead of the bloom of spring and summer, winter sets in, and stays. The lack of attention causes the decay of what was once so vibrant and healthy.

But, with a desire to change, the beauty can be regained. So long as the garden is nurtured, the years will bring radiance and flourish in richer shade.'

'Marriage is a commitment and relationship that starts in this Dunyā *(world) and will continue* inshā'Allāh *in Jannah together.'*

Dear groom,

Receive her heart in your hands,
Gently, not to crush it
Firmly, not to drop it
Constantly, not to abandon it

In infancy her heart was nourished in moonlit liquid feeds,
Cradled in arms joined to the hands of a clock
Enveloped in yarn from fields afar
Nurtured to fly with muslin woven wings.

Her youthful heart saw the planets in a raindrop
Felt the earth's rivers in the veins of a leaf,
Tasted the flavours of life in a pomegranate seed
Smelt a forest in a pine cone.

Hold her heart in your hands
Gently, firmly, constantly
For in holding her heart,
You carry ours too.

The bride's parents

The Eternal Sources

Marriage is part of the natural order on earth to achieve balance and harmony. God who is *al-Wadūd*, the Loving, sanctions the institution of marriage. It forms the cornerstone of communities across the world and through the ages.

And of everything We have created pairs that you may be mindful. (Surah *al-Dhāriyāt* 51:49)

It is He Who has created man from water, then established relationships of lineage and marriage: for your Sustainer is always able to do as He wills. (Surah *al-Furqān* 25:54)

O humankind! Be conscious of your Sustainer, Who has created you out of one living entity, and out of it created spouses and out of the two spread abroad a multitude of men and women. And remain conscious of God, in whose name you demand your rights from one another, and of these ties of kinship. Indeed, God is ever watchful over you! (Surah *al-Nisā'* 4:1)

O humankind! We created you from a single [pair] of a male and a female, and made you into nations and tribes, that you may know one other. Indeed, the most honoured of you in the sight of Allah is the one who is most deeply conscious of God. And God has full knowledge and is well acquainted [with all things]. (Surah *al-Ḥujurāt* 49:13)

Marriage is strongly encouraged as a Sunnah of the Prophet ﷺ and a trust to uphold. The benefit is both for the couple and society.

'Three categories of people Allah has obliged Himself to help: a *mujāhid* or striver in His cause, a worker to pay his debt, and the one who wants to marry to live a chaste life.' (Tirmidhī)

'The Prophet ﷺ said, "Marriage is part of my way or Sunnah; so whosoever keeps away from my Sunnah is not of me."' (Muslim)

Let those who find not the wherewithal for marriage keep themselves chaste, until Allah gives them means out of His grace. (Surah *al-Nūr* 24:33)

Prophet Hūd's response to the people of 'Ād who challenged his call to faith, is an apt principle when looking for a suitable match:
'*I put my trust in God, my Lord and your Lord. There is no moving creature which He does not control. My Lord's way is straight.*' (Surah *Hūd* 11:56)

The first step towards a blessed and fulfilling married life is seeking a suitable partner. The foundation of God consciousness and faith is the premise for making a choice.

This day are [all] things good and pure made lawful unto you. The food of the people of the Book is lawful for you and yours is lawful for them. [Lawful for you in marriage] are chaste women who are believers, and chaste women among the people of the

Book revealed before your time, when you give them their due dowers, and desire chastity, not lewdness nor secret intrigues. If anyone rejects faith, fruitless is his work, and in the Hereafter he will be among the losers. (Surah *al-Māʾidah* 5:5)

Women of purity are for men of purity, and men of purity are for women of purity. (Surah *al-Nūr* 24:26)

'The Prophet Muhammad ﷺ said: "Men choose women for four reasons: for their wealth, for their social standing, for their beauty and for their religion. But marry one who is religious and you will succeed."' (Bukhārī)

'The Messenger of God ﷺ said: "Not one of you should meet a woman alone unless she is accompanied by a relative within the prohibited degrees of marriage."' (Bukhārī)

The marriage contract, the strong covenant in this life and the hereafter is an act of worship, rewarded by *al-Wakīl*, the Trustee, *al-Raḥmān*, the Most Gracious. The Prophet's wedding sermon is in essence a call for the couple to make God-consciousness – *taqwā* – the foundation of their marriage. It is a reminder of their purpose of life, their accountability, their conduct with one another and the extended family. A marriage built with these bricks can pave the way to Jannah.

The Prophet's wedding sermon

> All praise and gratitude is for Allah. We seek
> guidance and forgiveness from Him. We also seek
> refuge in Him from the evils of our own selves.
> Whoever Allah guides, no one can misguide him.
> Whoever He lets go astray no one can put him
> back on track. We testify that there is no god but
> Allah and we testify that Muhammad is Allah's
> servant and His messenger.

After this initial statement, the Prophet ﷺ would recite the
following verses from the Qur'an:

> *Believers! Be conscious of Allah with all the
> consciousness that is due to Him, and see that you
> do not die except in the state of submission to Allah.*
> (Surah *Āl 'Imrān* 3:102)

> *O people! Be conscious of your Sustainer Who created
> you from a single entity and from this entity created
> its spouse; and out of the two spread many men and
> women. Be conscious of Allah in Whose name you
> seek rights from one another, and heed the ties of
> kinship. Surely, Allah is ever watchful over you.*
> (Surah *al-Nisā'* 4:1)

> *O believers, fear Allah and say what is sound and
> proper. Allah will set aright your deeds and will
> forgive your errors. Whoever obeys Allah and His
> Messenger, has indeed attained a great success.*
> (Surah *al-Aḥzāb* 33:70–71) (Tirmidhī)

Every relationship requires effort and investment from both parties. Working daily at this partnership is fluid. Unlike other types of work, success is not about fixed roles and fixed outcomes; on the contrary, it is about interchanging, flexibility, a willingness to adjust our steps as and when required. None of this 'work' is captured through filtered images of 'moments'. When the aim of the marriage is mutual comfort and tranquillity, then that is the direction both must walk in, together.

And among His wondrous signs is that He created spouses for you from among yourselves that you may find rest in them, and He put between you love and compassion; most surely there are signs in this for a people who reflect. (Surah *al-Rūm* 30:21)

'The Prophet Muhammad ﷺ was reported to have said: "The most perfect Muslim in the matter of faith is one who has excellent behaviour; and the best among you are those who behave best towards their wives."' (Tirmidhī)

'When 'Ā'ishah ؓ was asked what the Prophet ﷺ was like at home, she said: "He does what you all do in your houses – he also patches his clothes and repairs his shoes, and feeds his goats." He used to "serve his family", and help them in their household chores until the time came for Prayer, and then he would go out. There was no type of household work too low or too undignified for him.

'Ā'ishah, ؓ has stated: "He always joined in household work and would at times mend his clothes, repair his shoes and sweep the floor. He would milk, tether, and feed his animals and do the household shopping."' (Bukhārī)

'The day you married them (your wife), you considered them as a trust of Allah, and you brought them home according to His injunctions.'
(From the Prophet's Last Sermon)

'God's Messenger ﷺ said: "Indeed, Allah would say on the Day of Resurrection, 'Where are those who have mutual love for My Glory's sake? Today I shall shelter them in My shade when there is no shade but Mine'." (Bukhārī)

'The Prophet of God ﷺ said: "Keeping good company is like sitting with someone who carries musk. Keeping bad company is like sitting with someone who blows on coals. Good company lets you enjoy the pleasant scent even if you yourself do not carry it. Bad company is detrimental in two ways: you will either burn your clothes or smell bad."' (Bukhārī)

Kind words and forgiving faults are better than giving in charity. Allah is al-Ghanī, *Self-Sufficient, Forebearing.*
(Surah *al-Baqarah* 2:263)

'Messenger of Allah (ﷺ) said, "On the Day of Resurrection, Allah, the Exalted, will say: 'Where are those who have mutual love for the sake of My Glory? Today I shall shelter them in My Shade when there will be no shade except Mine'."' (Muslim)

Allah praised Zakariyah and his wife

*They used to hasten to do good deeds and would call on Us
with hope and fear, and used to humble themselves before Us.*
(Surah *al-Anbiyā'* 21:90)

**Justice is enjoined on each and every believer, and
upholding mutual obligations is an act of faith. For those
who have exhausted all avenues of making their marriage
work, the option of terminating the contract is permitted.**

*If a wife fears cruelty or desertion on her husband's part, there is
no blame on them if they arrange an amicable settlement between
themselves; and such a settlement is best, even though human
inner selves are swayed by greed. But if you do good and practise
self-restraint, Allah is well-acquainted with all that you do.*
(Surah *al-Nisā'* 4:128)

*O you who believe! Stand firmly for justice, as witnesses to Allah,
even against yourselves, or your parents, or your kin, and whether
it be [against] rich or poor; for Allah can best protect both. Follow
not the lusts [of your hearts], lest ye swerve, and if you distort
[justice] or decline to do justice, indeed Allah is well-acquainted
with all that you do.* (Surah *al-Nisā'* 4:135)

*O you who believe! You are forbidden to inherit women against
their will. Nor should you treat them with harshness, that you may
take away part of the dower you have given them – except where
they have been guilty of open lewdness – on the contrary, live with
them on a footing of kindness and equity. If you take a dislike to
them it may be that you dislike something through which Allah
brings about a great deal of good.* (Surah *al-Nisā'* 4:19)

Marriage is the foundation of a wider thriving family life from which grows reciprocal rights and responsibilities across the generations. When this foundation is strong, the rest of society has a firm base to build upon.

The believers, men and women, are protectors of one another. (Surah *al-Tawbah* 9:71)

'Each one of you is a trustee (shepherd) and is accountable for that which is entrusted to him. A ruler is a trustee and is accountable for his trust, a man is a trustee in respect of his family, a woman is a trustee in respect of her husband's property and children.' (Muslim)

God has given you spouses of your own kind, and has given you through your spouses, children and grandchildren, and has provided you sustenance out of the good things of life. Will people then continue to believe in what is false and deny God's favours? (Surah *al-Naḥl* 16:72)

'Whoever would like his sustenance to be increased, and to be blessed in his lifespan, should maintain good ties with his relatives.' (Bukhārī and Muslim)

Du'ā's for Married Life

These supplications guide us towards the purpose of marriage and remind us of the values that matter. In a world where appearances and superficial measures are used to supposedly 'guide' couples, we need to keep the essence of these words close to heart, to keep our expectations and focus real. The longing of the heart and soul: to find a suitable spouse, to live in a peaceful union, to be blessed with righteous lineage, are timeless needs addressed through the *du'ā's*. They help us to replace artificiality with simplicity and the temporal with the ever-lasting.

Prayer for newlyweds

'May Allah bless you, and shower His blessings upon you, and join you together in goodness.'

It is He Who created you all from a single entity. From this entity, He created its spouse in order that man might dwell with her [in love]. When they are united, she bears a light burden [the embryo] and carries it about [unnoticed]. When she grows heavy, they both pray to Allah their Sustainer, [saying]: 'If You give us a righteous child, we vow we shall be [ever] grateful.' (Surah *al-A'rāf* 7:189)

And grant, our Sustainer, that they enter the Gardens of Eternity which You have promised them, and to the righteous among their fathers, their wives, and their progeny! For You are the Exalted in Might, Full of Wisdom. (Surah *al-Mu'min* 40:8)

[And those who pray]: 'Our Sustainer! Grant unto us spouses and offspring who will be the delight of our eyes, and give us (the grace) to lead the righteous.' Those are the ones who will be rewarded with the highest place in heaven, because of their constant patience. Therein shall they be met with salutations and peace. (Surah *al-Furqān* 25:74–75)

'On the authority of Anas ﷺ the Prophet ﷺ heard someone supplicating to Allah saying:

"O Allah! I ask You that all praise is Yours. There is no true god except You, You are al-Mannān,[1][*] *the Originator of the Heavens and Earth, Possessor of Majesty and Honour. O the Ever-Living, O Self-Subsisting".*

The Prophet ﷺ then said: "He has supplicated to Allah using His Greatest Name; when supplicated with this Name, He answers, and when asked with this name He gives.'"
(*Sunan* Abū Dāwūd)

For the home:

'The Prophet ﷺ said: "Indeed, Allah wrote in a book two thousand years before He created the heavens and the earth, and He sent down two *āyāt* from it to end Surat *al-Baqarah* with. If they are recited for three nights in a home, no Shaytan shall come near it.'" (Tirmidhī)

---

1 [*] *Al-Mannān* (the Beneficent Bestower of bounties), the One such that all favours and blessings originate from Him, He is the One Who granted them and favoured the creation with them.

'The Prophet ﷺ said: "Recite Surat *al-Ikhlāṣ* and *Al-Mu'awwidhatayn* (Surat *al-Falaq* and Surat *al-Nās*) three times at dawn and dusk. It will suffice you in all respects."' (Abū Dāwūd)

Constant in Her Support,
A Partner of Distinction

Khadījah al-Kubrā 🌸: Khadījah the Great. Mother of the believers and wife of the noble Prophet of Allah 🌸

The noble lady Khadījah 🌸 was widowed twice before her marriage to Muhammad 🌸. He was fifteen years younger than she was but their marriage was a partnership of noble minds and hearts, for a task that was to change the course of human history.

Khadījah loved her husband dearly. His beautiful manners, his gentleness and generosity and his widespread reputation for honesty and trustworthiness, all formed the basis for her proposal to him. They shared marital harmony for twenty-three years and her admiration for him only increased as she witnessed his deep contemplative nature that unfolded before her eyes.

Khadījah 🌸 was accustomed to her husband going away to stay on mount Ḥirāʾ, overlooking the outskirts of Makkah. Leaving the bustling city of Makkah, he removed himself from all the concerns that engage mortal flesh in its daily routines. The retreat was made to nurture his spirit and for contemplation. In isolation, he spent the days and nights surrounded only by the firmament, the colossal rocks, mountains and the desert sands of the valleys. He was profoundly disturbed by the idol worship and the injustices that were part of the 'life' which the masses were simply 'living'.

In recent months, his need for solitude became more pressing. It was the month of Ramadan in the year 610 CE that Khadījah's husband ventured out into the emptiness of the valley, to climb the steep mountains. As always she supported him in every way she could. Her male servants carried supplies up the rocky tract and brought her back news of how he fared.

This particular evening after the sunset on the brow of the valley, her husband returned in an agitated state. His demeanour had visibly altered, as though he had been chased down the rocky tract; he was clearly unsettled. Thoughts and questions rolled around in her mind as to what could have happened to him.

Khadījah ﷺ always knew the Messenger of Allah ﷺ to be composed, measured and balanced, even in his very gait. On this evening, it was as though he had been touched by something from beyond the veils of the dark night. She took her shawl, as he had asked, and covered him with it. Did he have a fever, or had some illness overtaken him? Her embrace comforted him, and he began to speak of the events of this 'night of power'. She listened to what her husband related to her: how the angel of revelation, Jibrīl (Gabriel), had appeared to him on the horizon, how he had instructed Muhammad ﷺ to 'read' even though he could not, and how the figure conveyed to him the first words of the Qur'an, signifying that he was to be the chosen Messenger of God.

The years of retreating for periods of seclusion had reached their climax and their purpose was now apparent. This summons by the angel Jibrīl marked the beginning: the retreats had been a prelude to this call to Prophethood. The heavens had opened and called on the chosen one of God to commence his mission and set foot upon the earth anew, 'in the name of Allah'.

The noble Prophet's words fell on her fertile heart and deep conviction took root immediately. The lady Khadījah's intelligence, wisdom and her knowledge of her husband's character were sufficient to make an independent choice – and she chose to accept the final message of God. Although the blessed Prophet was initially confounded by the extraordinary nature of his experience, she reassured him with the following words:

'Never! By Allah, Allah will never disgrace you. You keep good relations with your kith and kin, help the poor and the destitute, serve your guests generously and assist the deserving calamity-afflicted ones.'

Thus was the lady Khadījah 🌸 the first believer in this final message from God – Islam. She submitted completely to the One, Almighty God, Sovereign and Sustainer of all. Soon after, she set off to see an elderly cousin named Waraqah ibn Nawfal – known for his perception, his rejection of idolatry, and being a believer in One God. She related the night's experience to him, and after listening to the account, he reassured her of the following:

'By Him in Whose hand is the soul of Waraqah, if what you say is true, there has come to Muhammad the great Nāmūs, even he who came to Moses. Truly Muhammad is the Prophet of this people. Calm your husband's fears and banish your own!'

Henceforth, the lady Khadījah 🌸 continued to be the emotional anchor for her husband, and did not stop at supporting him simply as a wife. She invested all her wealth and connections to deliver the message of believing in the One God, assisting in every way she could. Her endeavours contributed to laying the foundation of Islam, from which the message was to reach all corners of the world. She sacrificed her personal comforts as well and suffered alongside the small, yet growing, number of believers in Makkah. She was known as the patron of the poor, and found contentment in giving to those in need. The initial ten years of Prophethood were some of the toughest, and needed equally valiant pillars to support the Prophet ﷺ in the task that lay ahead of him.

The year in which the noble lady died became known as the 'Year of Sadness'. She passed away to the Mercy of God in the year 620 CE. She had shared a quarter of a century as the wife of Rasūlullāh – the Messenger of God – and was the mother of their seven children. His love and affection for her, however, never died and he would speak of her frequently, in addition to sending food and greetings to her friends who outlived her. Reminiscing some years after she passed away, he spoke from the heart:

'She believed in me when no one else did, she embraced Islam when people disbelieved me and she helped and comforted me when there was none to lend a helping hand.'

The passing away of this great and devoted wife and believer by no means meant the end of her legacy. The foundations she helped to lay in the first ten years of Prophethood were the basis for the spread of Islam across the globe. Though she has left this world, her destiny is known to us, and was made known to her in her lifetime:

The angel Jibril came to the Prophet ﷺ and said,

'O Allah's Apostle! This is Khadījah coming to you with a dish… When she reaches you, greet her on behalf of her Sustainer and on my behalf, and give her the glad tidings of having a palace of '*Qaṣab*' in Paradise wherein there will be neither any noise nor any fatigue (trouble).' (Bukhārī)

Motherhood
Raindrops

*And We have enjoined on man [to be good] to his parents:
in travail upon travail did his mother bear him, and his
weaning lasted two years. [We ask him]: 'Show gratitude to
Me and to thy parents. To Me is thy final goal.'*
(Surah *Luqmān* 31:14)

Motherhood

Mothering is an honour. Biological or not, the many ways a person is mothered – be it through their parents, grandparents, foster parents, adoptive mother, a neighbour, or sibling – all draw from the same font of love and commitment. A mother commits, a mother gives and a mother sacrifices. Add to these reams of other qualities and still the mother's role goes beyond definition. We can try and gather together the qualities that make this role so valuable but they are too numerous, like trying to count grains of sand along the coastline.

Being endowed with the miracle of carrying new life, then nurturing that life into maturity, is a milestone in the life of a woman. The respect conferred on mothers' is found in the Divine words of the Qur'an from *al-Raḥīm*, the Most Merciful, Compassionate, *al-Ḥaqq*, the Truth.

Being responsible for the care and development of new hearts and minds is a challenging role for which we are accountable. In our hands are placed the next inheritors of this planet, the next upholders of truth, and a new generation either in touch with their souls, or not. God willing, the benefits of fulfilling this role are reaped in this life and the next.

As a mother, or mother-to-be, you may receive many messages of how to prepare for this role. From the Qur'anic models, patience and self-sacrifice are two of the qualities that are most needed even before the birth takes place. As time goes on, and the demands upon you increase, you need to invest in your own self in order to have the strength, knowledge and understanding from which to give.

Maternal feelings are natural and a part of the genetic make up of a woman. Where there is conflict about accepting this role, external opinions are often the problem, not 'motherhood' itself. It is an anomaly that a role of such high esteem in the Qur'an and Sunnah is belittled and dismissed by society, the more advanced it becomes. In today's world, regrettably, motherhood translates as 'doing nothing', as being unproductive. Rather than being consumed by the doubts and uncertainties which plague the modern-day mother, this is a stage in life that needs to be celebrated and embraced, accepted and respected primarily by ourselves – those who fulfil the role of mothering.

Raindrops fall, life continues as it soaks into the ground drenching the soil. Rainfall beats without hesitation or questions. Its rhythm varies; now a gushing flow, then a faint drip, drip, drip, measured in time. Rain is an unending dance, a poem, a painting, a translucent mosaic. Of all the waters in our world, these simple, crystal-like drops sustain life. Some drops nourish the ground, others trickle down slopes, forming streams which flow to make rivers, which in turn make their way to the sea. So too with motherhood: it is the source of feeding lives that one day become part of the great seas of this world, covering the surface of the earth.

Myriad Voices

'I celebrate all the blessings I have been endowed with. To receive God's creation, placed in my care, is a great honour. It is a responsibility I am given, and I am accountable for my part in shaping the next generation.'

'I wonder when it all happened.
Which curtain was lifted for me to walk into this part?
Which morning did I awaken to the title of 'mother'?
When did I transform from having one breath and one heart to having two?
Which ocean did I sail, or terrain cross to reach this new land of Motherhood?And now, having arrived here, where is my map and guide to show me the way?
How will I fare? Am I really equipped?'

'I work and strive towards producing inheritors of the earth who will care for it, invest in it and tread it carefully on the way to their eternal home.'

'To thrive and grow as a mother, the person inside needs to be cared for, nourished, and invested in. Only when the fountain of energy, creativity and patience are replenished can the productive maternal force flow forth.'

'At the end of the day, when I have to scrape the bottom of my emotional barrel for strength and perseverance, I remember that my '*possessions and children are a test, and that with Allah is a mighty reward.*' (Surah *al-Anfāl* 8:28)

'Each day requires the skills of a nurse,
the patience of an educator,
the planning of a manager,
the creativity and vision of an artist
and the wisdom of a sage from centuries past.
So, when you next face me, from across a desk, somewhere,
please do not stare blankly when I answer "I am a mother",
and reiterate louder "So *what* do you do?"'

'Everyone reminisces about their childhood. Some look back with pleasure, others pain, most a combination of the two. I hold a child's past in my hands today. What they will look back on is the business of my daily life now. My role in shaping and colouring their lives will be the content of their memory.'

'Motherhood is
the making
of history,
each and every day.'

'Am I "me" or am I "*her*", the one they look up to,
call out to,
hold on to,
imitate, and address as their "mama"?
If I am "*her*",
then where did "I" go
and when will we meet?'

'The drops that gush
The drops that fall
The drops that trickle
Are the drops that nourish
Are the drops that feed
Are the drops that carry
The transparent life-force
Inside each of us.

Raindrops grow forests
Tear drops grow compassionate souls.
May both flow,
And feed the soil and soul,
One letter apart
"i" and "u" together.
Stronger'

"'Motherhood", she said "is a cycle of learning and then unlearning. It's like this: first you learn commitment and care, watching your helpless baby, protecting them – this is survival. Then you teach: sounds, words, actions and repeat. Repeat until they learn – this is instruction. Soon they are independent, and you walk beside them. It may take a decade, it may take two, but in their own time they will take the reins in their own hands, while you stay nearby, to steady, to catch, to fill in the gaps. This all happens at the 'motherhood school'. You're at ease now, this school is familiar, its surroundings and its ways; you are comfortable.

"Just then, it happens. One morning, or one night, you don't know exactly when, you need to move to the unlearning part. You need to stop watching them all the time, for their survival. You need to step back and give them space to make their way ahead, far ahead, as you recede; now a shrinking shadow blended into the background of an impressionist landscape.

"While unlearning, you need to say less and listen more. Move from the sidelines to the spectator's seat. Unravel the ball of wool, erase the lines, un-learn the skills you honed for so long and so well; past diligence is misplaced now. They need to make the marks, the pen is in their hands and they will write you into their chapters, just like you wrote them into yours.'"

Motherhood Rain

I fall between the cracks
That's where I settle
Where rain gathers
On the pavements of this world
Daily
Unnoticed
I fall between the cracks.

Who is a mother?
A being in motion
A downpour of raindrops racing to reach
The concrete slabs labelled
'Caring and nurturing'
'Professional and official'
'Home maker and domestic'
'Academic and activist'
'Adventurous and outgoing'
'Best friend and confidant'
'Independent and autonomous'
'Organiser and mentor'.

I fall between the cracks.
On Monday I was a light shower,
Splashed over
Nurturing but not adventurous
Activist but not professional
Caring but not domestic.

I fall between the cracks.
On Tuesday I was torrential rain,
Gushed down on

Domestic but not best friend
Professional but not mentor
Organiser but not independent.

By Sunday I had gathered.
Collected in a pool of freshwater glistening
In a garden pot
I liked its shape and filled it.
Not falling between anything
The pot had a label:
'Nameless and Whole'.

The Eternal Sources

The gift of a new life arrives solely from the permission of Allah – Who is *al-Muṣawwir*, the Fashioner, and *al-Badī'*, the Originator. Only God alone decides when a boy or girl will enter this world and to whom this is granted.

To God belongs the dominion of the heavens and the earth. He creates what He wills, He bestows [children] male or female according to His Will, or He bestows both males and females, and He leaves barren whom He wills; for He is full of Knowledge and Power. (Surah *al-Shūrā* 42:49–50)

And God created you from dust, then from a drop, then He made you into pairs. And no female carries or gives birth without His knowledge. And no one grows old among those who become old, nor is anything lessened of his term, without its being in a Book [of decrees]. Truly, that is easy for Allah. (Surah *Fāṭir* 35:11)

'The Prophet ﷺ said: "At every womb Allah appoints an angel who says, 'O Sustainer! A drop of semen, O Sustainer! A clinging fertilized ovum. O Sustainer! A little lump of flesh.' Then if Allah wishes (to complete) its creation, the angel asks, '(O Sustainer!) Will it be a male or female, wretched or blessed, and how much will his provision be? And what will his age be?' So all that is written while the child is still in the mother's womb.'" (Bukhārī)

It is He Who created for you the faculties of hearing, sight, feeling and understanding. Yet you are seldom grateful. (Surah *al-Mu'minūn* 23:78)

*And God brought you forth from your mothers' wombs knowing
nothing, and then He has endowed you with hearing, sight and
minds so that you may be grateful to Him.* (Surah *al-Naḥl* 16:78)

'God's Messenger ﷺ said: "Indeed, Allah created on the same
day when He created the heavens and the earth, one hundred
parts of mercy. Every part of mercy is analogous to the space
between the heavens and the earth, and out of this mercy He
endowed one part to the earth and it is because of this that the
mother shows affection to her child."' (Muslim)

*It is He Who created you all from a single entity. From this entity,
He created its spouse in order that man might dwell with her [in
love]. When they are united, she bears a light burden [the embryo]
and carries it about [unnoticed]. When she grows heavy, they both
pray to Allah their Sustainer, [saying]: 'If You give us a righteous
child, we vow we shall be [ever] grateful.'* (Surah *al-Aʿrāf* 7:189)

**Pregnancy and motherhood bring an array of physical
and emotional hurdles with them. These challenges
can overwhelm new mothers without support and care.
Alongside practical help, it is a comfort to know that every
atom's worth of struggle and effort a mother experiences is
rewarded by *al-Raḥmān, al-Raḥīm*, the All Compassionate,
the Most Merciful. No endeavour is overlooked by Him.**

*We have enjoined on man to be kind to his parents. In pain
did his mother bear him, and in pain did she give birth to him.*
(Surah *al-Aḥqāf* 46:15)

'Narrated by Anas, Sallamah – the nurse of his son Ibrāhīm – said to the Prophet ﷺ, "You brought tidings of all good things to men."

The Prophet ﷺ said, "Does it not please any one of you that if a woman is pregnant by her husband and he is satisfied with her that she receives the reward of one who fasts and prays for the sake of Allah? And when the labour pains come no one in heaven or earth knows what is concealed in her womb to soothe her (cool her eyes). And when she delivers, not a mouthful of milk flows from her and not an instance of the child's suck, but that she receives, for every mouthful and for every suck, the reward of one good deed. And if she is kept awake by her child at night, she receives the reward of one who frees seventy slaves for the sake of Allah.'" (Ṭabarānī)

'The Prophet ﷺ said, "A woman who dies in childbirth together with the baby becomes a martyr."' (Aḥmad)

Every act with the intention to please Allah *subḥānahu wa taʿālā* is rewardable, including the time and effort given in maintaining one's family. When the mother spends from her own wealth on her family and children, she is rewarded. At the same time, we are reminded of keeping a balance, in order that love and commitment to one's family doesn't take precedence over our remembrance and commitment to *al-Wahhāb*, the Bestower.

'Of the dinar you spend in God's path or to set free a slave or as a charity given to a needy person or to support your family, the one yielding the greatest reward is that which you spend on your family.' (Muslim)

'The Messenger of Allah ﷺ instructed me to do ten things, (and among them was): "spend on your children according to your means."' (Aḥmad)

'A woman asked the Prophet ﷺ: "O Messenger of Allah, shall I be rewarded if I spend to provide for Abū Salama's sons (presumably after Abū Salama's death), when they are my sons as well?" The Prophet ﷺ replied, "Spend on them, for you will get a reward for what you spend on them."' (Bukhārī)

'Zaynab, the wife of 'Abdullāh ibn Mas'ūd, used to provide for 'Abdullāh and those orphans who were under her protection. She enquired of the Prophet ﷺ whether it was permissible for her to spend from her zakat for them. "Yes," replied the Prophet ﷺ, 'and you will receive a double reward: one for helping relatives and the other for giving zakat."' (Bukhārī)

Your wealth and your children are only a test, while with Allah there is a tremendous reward. (Surah *al-Taghābun* 64:15)

O you who believe! Let not your wealth nor your children distract you from the remembrance of Allah. Those who do so are the losers. (Surah *al-Munāfiqūn* 63:9)

Though place and time may change, the elevated rank of parents, with a special place for the mother, remains unchanged. As parents become older, it is their right to receive respect and company. If it is written for us, we will experience how our roles orbit; born in need and then aging in need. Caring for elders paves a pathway to Jannah. Though this pathway is not guaranteed to be smooth and scenic, it is the most honourable.

Your Sustainer has decreed that you worship none but Him, and that you be kind to your parents. Whether one or both of them attain old age during your life, say not to them a word of contempt, nor repel them, but address them in terms of honour. And out of kindness, lower to them the wing of humility, and say: 'My Sustainer! Bestow on them both Your Mercy even as they cherished me in childhood.' (Surah *Banī Isrā īl* 17:23–24)

We have enjoined on man kindness to parents; but if [either of them] strive [to force] you to associate with Me anything of which you have no knowledge, do not obey them. (Surah *al-'Ankabūt* 29:8)

We have enjoined on man [to be good] to his parents... [We ask him]: 'Show gratitude to Me and to thy parents. To Me is thy final goal. But if they [parents] strive to make you associate in worship with Me things of which you have no knowledge, do not obey them. Yet bear them company in this life with goodness [and consideration] and follow the way of those who turn to Me.' (Surah *Luqmān* 31:14–15)

'Worship none save Allah and be good to parents...' (Surah *al-Baqarah* 2:83)

'The satisfaction of the Sustainer is in the satisfaction of the parents, and the displeasure of the Sustainer is in the displeasure of the parents.' (Tirmidhī)

From a longer hadith, the Prophet ﷺ said: 'Indeed, Allah forbade for you rudeness (disobedience) to mothers.' (Bukhārī)

'A man came to the Prophet ﷺ and said, "O Messenger of God! Who among the people is the most worthy of my good companionship?" The Prophet ﷺ said: "Your mother." The man said, "Then who?" The Prophet ﷺ said: "Then your mother." The man further asked, "Then who?" The Prophet ﷺ said: "Then your mother." The man asked again, "Then who?" The Prophet ﷺ said: "Then your father".' (Bukhārī)

'Abū Usayd al-Sāʿidī said: "We were once sitting with the Messenger of Allah ﷺ when a man from the tribe of Salmah came and said to him: 'O Messenger of Allah! Do my parents have rights over me even after they have died?' And the Messenger of Allah ﷺ said: 'Yes. You must pray to Allah to bless them with His forgiveness and mercy, fulfil the promises they made to anyone, and respect their relations and their friends'.'" (Abū Dāwūd)

'The Messenger of God ﷺ said: "The major sins are to believe that God has partners, to disobey one's parents, to commit murder, and to bear false witness."' (Bukhārī)

'Asmā' bint Abū Bakr ؓ narrated that during the treaty of Hudaybiyyah, her mother, who was then pagan, came to see her from Makkah. Asmā' informed the Messenger of Allah ﷺ of her arrival and also that she needed help. He said: "Be good to your mother".' (Muslim)

'The Prophet ﷺ said, "God has forbidden you to be undutiful to your mothers, to withhold (what you should give) or demand (what you do not deserve), and to bury your daughters alive. And God dislikes that you should talk too much about others, ask too many questions (in religion), or waste your property."' (Bukhārī)

'I asked the Prophet ﷺ, "Which deed is the dearest to Allah?"
He replied, "To offer the fixed Prayers at their early stated times."
I asked, "What is the next (in goodness)?"
He replied, "To be good and dutiful to your parents." I again
asked, "What is the next (in goodness)?"
He replied, "To participate in jihad in Allah's cause." Abdullah
added, "I asked only that much and if I had asked more, the
Prophet ﷺ would have told me more".' (Bukhārī)

'"Let him be humbled (let his pride be in the dust); let him be
humbled; let him be humbled." It was said, "O Messenger of
Allah ﷺ, who should be humiliated so?" He said, "He who
finds his parents in old age, either one of them or both of
them and does not enter Paradise by serving them."' (Muslim)

'The Prophet ﷺ said, "The word 'al-raḥm' (womb) derives its
name from 'al-Raḥmān' (i.e. Allah). So whosoever keeps good
relations with it (the womb, i.e. kith and kin), Allah will keep
good relations with him, and whosoever will sever it (i.e. severs
his bonds of kith and kin) Allah too will sever His relations
with him."' (Bukhārī)

Du‘ā's for parents and offspring

The relationship between parent and child is a place where many are tested, and we are forewarned about this in the sacred sources. The tests can be the hardest a parent or child faces, as the bond between them is like no other. These du‘as carry the coolness of gratitude and warmth of mercy into the believers' hearts. They reflect the reciprocal relationship between parent and child, where, one prays that mutual care will flow between them. Allah *subḥānahu wa ta‘ālā* is *al-Karīm*, the Bountiful, *al-Mu‘min*, the Giver of Security, and to Him do we turn for the wellbeing of this unique kinship.

'Our Sustainer! Forgive me and my parents and the believers on the Day of Reckoning.' (Surah *Ibrāhīm* 14:41)

Prophet Sulaymān ﷺ supplicated:
'My Sustainer! Inspire me to be thankful for the blessings You have granted me and my parents, and to do good deeds that please You; admit me by Your grace into the ranks of Your righteous servants.' (Surah *al-Naml* 27:19)

'My Sustainer! Forgive me and my parents and him who enters my house believing, and all believing men and believing women.' (Surah *Nūḥ* 71:28)

'Our Sustainer! Pour out on us patience and constancy, and make us die as those who have surrendered themselves unto You.' (Surah *al-A‘rāf* 7:126)

'Our Sustainer! Grant that our spouses and our offspring be a comfort to our eyes, and give us the grace to lead those who are conscious of You.' (Surah *al-Furqān* 25:74)

'My Sustainer! Bestow on them both Your Mercy even as they cherished me in childhood.' (Surah *Banī Isrā'īl* 17:24)

Prophet Ibrāhīm ﷺ to his father said, 'Peace be with you: I will beg my Lord to forgive you – He has always been kind to me. But for now I will leave you, and the idols you all pray to, and I will pray to my Lord and trust that my prayer will not be in vain.' (Surah *Maryam* 19:47–48)

'The Prophet ﷺ used to seek Refuge with Allah for al-Ḥasan and al-Ḥusayn and say: "Your forefather (i.e. Ibrāhīm) used to seek Refuge with Allah for Ishmā'īl and Isḥāq by reciting the following: 'O Allah! I seek Refuge with Your Perfect Words from every devil and from poisonous pests and from every evil, harmful, envious eye'".' (Bukhārī)

A Devout Mother,
A Historical Birth

The Blessed Maryam 🌸, mother of Prophet ʿĪsā 🌸

Maryam 🌸 was a woman whose life was dedicated to worship; she was the answer to her mother's supplication, she descended from the lineage of Prophet Dāʾūd 🌸 and was honoured with having the nineteenth Surah of the Qurʾan named after her: Surah *Maryam*.

Before birth, Maryam's life was vowed by her mother, Hanna, to be spent worshipping in Bayt al-Maqdis (Jerusalem). Under the guardianship of Prophet Zakariyah 🌸, the young girl grew into a beacon of righteousness and chastity. Before the narrative of her miraculous child-bearing is related, Maryam's youth is marked by her uncontested spiritual elevation as an example and a sign for all mankind.

The renowned narrative from the sacred sources on how she became a mother and bore the hardship that it entailed is central to the introduction of the great Prophet, ʿĪsā 🌸. He is known as 'ʿĪsā ibn Maryam' in the Qurʾan, the son of Mary, rather than Maryam 🌸, the mother of ʿĪsā. It is how Allah *subḥānahu wa taʿālā* chose to reveal the story that we learn of her immense courage, as a single mother, who shoulders the weight of her miraculous child-bearing alone. In Maryam 🌸 we find a young, spiritual, God-conscious mother whose legacy is timeless.

'The best of the women of the world are: "Maryam bint 'Imrān, Khadījah bint Khuwaylid, Fāṭimah bint Muhammad, and Āsiyah, the wife of Pharaoh".' (Tirmidhī)

'Behold!' the angels said, 'O Maryam! God has chosen you and purified you – chosen you above the women of all nations. O Maryam! Worship your Sustainer devoutly: Prostrate yourself, and bow down [in prayer] with those who bow.'
(Surah *Āl 'Imrān* 3:42–43)

And the angels said: 'O Maryam! God gives good news to you, through a word from Him, his name shall be Messiah, 'Īsā the son of Maryam. He shall be of great honour in this world and the Hereafter, and one of those brought near to God.'
(Surah *Āl 'Imrān* 3:45)

She said: 'O Sustainer! How can I have a child when no mortal hath touched me?' The angel replied, 'Thus it is. God creates what He wills. When He decrees a matter, He only says to it "Be", and it is.' (Surah *Āl 'Imrān* 3:47)

Recall in the Book [the story of] Maryam, when she withdrew from her family to a place in the east. She placed a screen [to hide herself] from them; then We sent her Our angel, and he appeared before her as a human being in all respects.
She said: 'I seek refuge from you in [Allah] Most Gracious: [come not near] if you fear Allah.' He said: 'I am only a messenger from your Sustainer, [to announce] to you the gift of a pure son.' 'How shall I have a son,' she said, 'seeing that no man has touched me, and I am not unchaste?' He said, 'So [will it be]: your Sustainer

*says: "That is easy for Me; and [We wish] to appoint him as a
Sign to people and a mercy from Us. It is a matter [so] decreed."'*

*So she conceived him, and she retired with him to a remote place.
And the pains of childbirth drove her to the trunk of a palm tree.
She cried [out in her anguish]: 'Ah! Would that I had died before
this! Would that I had been a thing forgotten!'
But [a voice] cried to her from beneath [the palm tree]: 'Grieve
not! For your Sustainer has provided a rivulet beneath you. And
shake towards yourself the trunk of the palm tree, it will let fall
fresh ripe dates upon you.
So eat and drink and cool [your] eye. And if you see any man, say,
"I have vowed a fast to [God] Most Gracious, and this day will I
enter into no talk with any human being."'*

*At length she brought the [baby] to her people, carrying him [in
her arms]. They said: 'O Maryam! Truly a strange thing have
you brought! O sister of Aaron! Your father was not a man of
evil, nor your mother a woman unchaste!' But she pointed to the
baby. They said: 'How can we talk to one who is a child in the
cradle?' He said: 'I am indeed a servant of Allah. He has given me
revelation and made me a Prophet; and He has made me blessed
wheresoever I may be, and has enjoined on me Prayer and Zakat
(charity) as long as I live.
[He has made me] kind to my mother, and not overbearing
or unblessed.
So peace is on me the day I was born, the day that I die, and the
day that I shall be raised up to life [again].'
Such [was] 'Īsā, the son of Maryam, and [it is] a statement of
truth, about which they [vainly] dispute.
It is not befitting to [the majesty of] Allah that He should beget a
son. Glory be to Him! When He determines a matter, He only says
to it, 'Be', and it is.*

['Īsā had said]: 'Verily, God is my Sustainer and your Sustainer, therefore worship Him [alone]. This is a Way that is straight.' (Surah *Maryam* 19:16–36)

The Age of Wisdom

Treasures in the Sea

It is He Who has created you all from dust, then from a sperm-drop, then from a leech-like clot; then does He get you out [into the light] as a child: then lets you [grow and] reach your age of full strength; then lets you become old, though of you there are some who die before; and lets you reach a term appointed, in order that you may learn wisdom. (Surah al-Mu'min 40:67)

The Age of Wisdom

As currents swell wave upon wave, moving in succession,
so do the stages of life come one upon each other, sooner than
expected. Each new wave holds strengths from our past,
whilst it surges ahead into the vast unknown. Likewise, our
journey into the stage of wisdom, or the *murabbī* –
the esteemed teacher as is often used in Muslim society –
brings with it a storehouse of experience, of burnished survival
and a deeper understanding of the workings of this world.
Reaching the sagacious age of an elder is at once an honour,
a test and blessing.

Having passed through decades experiencing the peaks and
troughs of life, this stage emerges shaped by experiences, like
the ridges on a cliff face carved by the crashing waves. This
graceful age is one that rests on the experience of feeling and
recognizing life's intricate patterns. It is a time when successes
and the fruits of one's labour can be savoured, whether far
from the crowd or in the pleasure of one's friends and family.

With all the stages of life we are destined to cross, there is the
inevitability of change. Change is often unwelcome; it can feel
uncomfortable and awkward, as is the case with all growth.
Some changes of this stage can be all the harder because roles
are renegotiated and needs redefined. Where once you were
the principal person who gave time, energy, guidance and
support, now in the reciprocal nature of relationships, this age
is a time to receive once again. You may receive time, affection
and care whilst you impart the valued gifts of perception and
hindsight. Relationships are reciprocal in theory, but in reality
this may not happen and so the shifting lines of rights and
responsibilities makes some relationships difficult to navigate.

For many this age is accompanied by grief. Loss of loved ones, unfulfilled dreams and loneliness can make daily life challenging. The tests of health, both on the body and mind can reach their climax as former strengths give way to new ailments. Yet, beneath everything, in holding onto one's faith there is comfort from *al-Salām*, the Source of Safety and Peace, and *al-Qawī*, the Strong.

On the surface, the oceans' appearance, like this stage of life, does not show what treasures it has beneath it, accumulating there for years. Yet below lies the magnificence of coral and the world of underwater life, growing silently over time. On the ocean floor rest the iridescent pearls, layer upon layer, hidden in the translucent sphere. Years have passed to create them, and those who seek such treasures will dive deep to retrieve them, while those who look to the surface will miss them.

Myriad Voices

'Who calls me "old"? What is "old"?
When the moon is full in numbers it is the subject of the
poet's verse,
When the herbs have matured they are the cook's pleasure.
When the trunk of a tree matures it is the carpenter's treasure,
When the gems of centuries past are retrieved they become
priceless exhibits.
"Old?" I call my age "precious".'

'I lean in the doorway where I once dashed in and out in haste.
In this house, on this street, under these telephone wires laid
down six decades ago.
"My home" now, once upon a time, "our home".
Through my frosted eyes I no longer see the neighbours,
Nor those paving stones or coral-pink rose gardens.
Change has swept through and left me in a new place beyond
this threshold.
The calendar sweeps up years of my life, gathered like auburn
leaves blown out of sight on an autumn afternoon; the days,
the months, the memories drift back into the soil.
New faces and new families turn the bricks and mortar into
their homes,
New chapters unfold under their slate tiles.
The loyal hazelnut tree remains with me –
This doorway, that tree and I, the three of us recognize
each other.'

'Once upon a time my table was always full.
Full of plates and food and children. Full of noise, talking,
bickering and laughter. My pots were busy, scarcely a chance
to sit idle between delivering sustenance, moving between fire
and water then fire again. Feeding so many; so many guests at
my table.
Years have gone by and, like stars vanish on a cloudy night, my
table has disappeared.
No longer laid full.
Lost. I search for it, but can't find those pots, plates or young
children anywhere. Somewhere in the distance I see new
tables unfolding. Each person is busy now laying their own
spreads. As I watch and rejoice as the new stoves are warming,
my heart still aches for that which was my own. The table has
disappeared, like the steam that rose from its dishes.
Too far away like a story of old.'

'Discovery is the name of my twilight years.
Discovering a new person emerging after my younger self is
spent, faded into multiple people's lives – dispersed to other
lands.
Discovering a new confidence after my former self has taken
a leap into free-fall and plunged straight into an oasis.
Discovering a new language after my script has finished.
Discovering new hands to fearlessly create without a need
or a purpose.
My twilight years; radiant and igniting, discovering discovery.'

'What meaning does the word "home" have now?
When I was young, my spouse and I built a home; we
nurtured, protected, warmed and cared for those in our home,
a place where each person had a place. Familiar objects, voices
and routines, encased in mutual love, was our home.
Now this cold, clinical building, where I am a number and a
visitor, I am told is also a "home".
What is a "home"?'

The Eternal Sources

It is the plan of *al-Khāliq*, the Creator, in His infinite Wisdom that all living things start from a seed, grow through stages, maturing, until an appointed time. Just as the bloom of summer is followed by shedding and slowing of autumn, so the winter of our lives brings us back to our roots, our core. Without the foliage yet comfortable in our reality. Ageing isn't fought and delayed, but welcomed as the natural process, the pattern we see all around us.

O mankind! If you have a doubt about Resurrection, [consider] that We created you out of dust, then out of sperm, then out of a leech-like clot, then out of a morsel of flesh, partly-formed and partly-unformed, in order that We may manifest [Our power] to you. And We cause whom We will to rest in the wombs for an appointed term, then do We bring you out as babies, then [foster you] that you may reach your age of full strength. Some of you are called to die, and some are sent back to the feeblest old age, so that they know nothing after having known [much], and gone [further]. You see the earth barren and lifeless, but when We pour down rain upon it, it is stirred [into life], swells and puts forth every kind of beautiful growth. (Surah *al-Ḥajj* 22:5)

If We extend anyone's life, We reverse his development. Do they still not use their reason? (Surah *Yā Sīn* 36:68)

This is the stage of life that society should elevate. In societies where the elders are honoured and coveted as a source of blessing, the idea of suppressing this stage is alien. When the elderly are on the fringes of society, treated as a burden, the landscape looks desolate and uninviting and so trying to escape it becomes the norm. We are reminded in clear terms what the standard towards the elderly is: honour and humility.

Your Sustainer has decreed that you worship none but Him, and that you be kind to your parents. Whether one or both of them attain old age during your life, say not to them a word of contempt, nor repel them, but address them in terms of honour. And out of kindness, lower to them the wing of humility, and say: 'My Sustainer! Bestow on them both Your Mercy even as they cherished me in childhood.'

Your Sustainer knows best what is in your hearts. If you do deeds of righteousness, indeed He is Most Forgiving to those who turn to Him again and again [in true penitence].
(Surah *Banī Isrā'īl* 17:23–25)

'The Messenger of Allah ﷺ said: "The finest act of goodness on the part of a son is to treat kindly the loved ones of his father."' (Muslim)

'He who likes that his sustenance should be expanded and his age may be lengthened should maintain the ties of kinship.' (Muslim)

As with the previous stages in life, the tests and difficulties that befall the elderly can seem all the more crushing, given one's fragility – physically and mentally. Whatever the array of difficulties that touch their lives, these too can be a means of drawing closer to *al-Ra'ūf*, the Compassionate. There is comfort in knowing God is *al-Qarīb*, the Near.

'I was with the Prophet ﷺ and some Arabs came to him asking: "O Messenger of Allah: Do we take medicine for treatment?" He said: "Yes, O you servants of Allah, take medicine, as Allah Almighty has not created a disease without having created a cure for it except one disease." They asked, "What is that?" He said: "Old age."' In another saying: 'Allah never inflicts a disease without providing a cure…' (Ibn Mājah)

'The Prophet ﷺ said, "No fatigue, nor disease, nor sorrow, nor sadness, nor hurt, nor distress befalls a Muslim, even if it were the prick he receives from a thorn, but that Allah expiates some of his sins for that."' (Bukhārī)

Advancing age increases perception. While the physical eyes may be in decline the inner eyes see the world and our place in it with new clarity. The transitory nature of this life now stands out like a lighthouse on a stormy night, high above the thrusting waves. Its light shines far and reveals the deep waters of this world for what they are – a source of sustenance or a place of drowning.

What is the life of this world but amusement and play? But certainly, the home in the Hereafter is life indeed, if they but knew. (Surah *al-'Ankabūt* 29:64)

One day He will gather them together, and [it will be] as if they had not stayed [in the life of this world] but for an hour of a day… (Surah *Yūnus* 10:45)

Blessed be He who has the dominion of the Universe in His Hand,
for He has power over all things.
He Who created death and life to test which of you is best in
action. He is the Almighty, the Ever Forgiving.
(Surah *Mulk* 67:1–2)

**It is natural that the passage into the next life is at the
forefront of the elderly person's mind. The pain of
knowing familiar faces, companions from that far off land
of youth, are no longer there for long conversations. The
memories of parents held in the heart and on faded photos
in albums are constant reminders that the next stage is
near, that this life is indeed a journey. That the soul's
eternal existence is edging towards a new place, a new time.
As long as there is life there is hope, there is still time to
gain closeness to *al-Shakūr,* the Appreciative, *Khayru-n-
Nāṣirīn,* the Best of Helpers. (Surah *Al 'Imrān* 3:150)**

'There was a group of My servants who said, "Our Sustainer, we
have īmān, so forgive us and have mercy on us. You are the Best of
the Merciful." But you made a mockery of them so that you forgot
Me while you were laughing at them.
Today I have rewarded them for being steadfast. They are the ones
who are victorious.'
Then He will ask them, 'How many years did you tarry on the
earth?' They will say, 'We tarried there for a day or part of a day.
Ask those who are able to count!' He will say, 'You only tarried
there for a little while if you did but know! Did you suppose that
We created you for amusement and that you would not return to
Us?' (Surah *al-Mu'minūn,* 23:109–115)

Whatever you have been given is only the enjoyment of the life of this world. What is with God is better and longer lasting for those who have faith and trust in their Sustainer.
(Surah *al-Shūrā* 42:36)

Yet still you prefer the life of this world when the Hereafter is better and longer lasting. (Surah *al-Aʿlā* 87:16–17)

O you who believe! Let not your riches or your children divert you from the remembrance of Allah. If any act thus, the loss is their own.

And spend [in charity] out of the sustenance that We have bestowed on you, before death should come to any of you and he should say: 'O my Sustainer! Why did You not give me respite for a little while? I should then have given [more] in charity, and I should have been one of the doers of good?' But Allah will grant respite to no soul when the time appointed [for it] has come. Allah is well acquainted with [all] that you do.
(Surah *al-Munāfiqūn* 63:9–11)

*Duʿāʾ*s for God's Grace and Mercy

'O Allah! I seek refuge with You from decrepitude and laziness, cowardice and miserliness. I seek refuge with You from afflictions of life and death and seek refuge with You from the punishment in the grave.' (Bukhārī)

'O Allah! I seek Your refuge from incapacity, laziness, cowardice, miserliness, decrepit old age, and punishment of the grave. O Allah! Grant my soul its dutifulness (*taqwā*), and purify it, You are the One to purify it; You are its Guardian and its Lord. O Allah! I seek Your refuge from knowledge that does not benefit, and from a heart that is not humble, and from a soul that is never satisfied, and from a supplication that is not answered.' (Aḥmad)

'O Allah! Wash away my sins with the water of snow and hail, and cleanse my heart from all the sins as a white garment is cleansed from the filth, and let there be a long distance between me and my sins, as You made East and West far from each other.' (Bukhārī)

'*My Lord! My bones have grown feeble and my head is glistening with age; yet, never have my prayers to You, my Lord, been unfruitful.*' (Surah *Maryam* 19:4)

'O Allah, I ask, Oh Allah, You are the One,
the Only, Self-Sufficient Master, Who was
not Begotten and Begets not, And none
is equal to Him, Forgive me my sins,
surely You are Forgiving, Merciful.'
(Aḥmad)

'O Allah, Grant health to my body. Oh Allah,
Grant health to my hearing. Oh Allah,
Grant health to my sight.'
(Abū Dāwūd)

'O Allah, Help me to Remember You, and Thank You,
and Worship You in the best of manners.' (Muslim)

A Lifetime of Commitment and Devotion, Caring for the Prophet ﷺ with Maternal Warmth

Barakah ﷺ: A lady of Paradise

The terrain from Makkah to Madinah was difficult to cross. Gruelling heat in the day and freezing temperatures at night were the constant backdrops to the stony desert tracts that seemed to lead to nowhere. Crossing this, however, was the now elderly Barakah ﷺ, well into her sixties as she made her journey to join the Muslims in Madinah.

When she finally arrived, the journey had taken its toll. Barakah's feet were swollen and she was exhausted. On seeing her condition, her beloved 'son' greeted her and hastened to help her and make her comfortable.

'*Yā Umm Ayman, Yā Ummī!* O my mother! Indeed for you is a place in Paradise.'

These words were spoken by Muhammad ﷺ, the gentle, compassionate Prophet of God, and the one who had been put in Barakah's care since his infancy.

Barakah's relationship with the Prophet ﷺ was unique. She was there to care for his mother when she carried him; she was there at his birth. Through his childhood years, moving between the homes of grandfather and uncle, Barakah ﷺ never left the young Muhammad ﷺ. Even after his marriage, she stayed in the home of Muhammad and Khadījah, peace and blessings be upon them both. But she had her own family too. She had two sons, Ayman and Usāmah, and was known as 'Umm Ayman' – the Mother of Ayman.

Growing older, however, never deterred her constant support for Islam and the noble Prophet ﷺ whom she loved as a son. Her life in Madinah was tied to the efforts of establishing and spreading the message of God. Her courage spurred her beyond the boundaries of age as she played an active role in battles, particularly the Battle of Uḥud by tending to the wounded and providing them with water.

'I shall never leave him,' Barakah ؓ often said, and she lived out her statement. When the Prophet ﷺ went on expeditions she often accompanied him, to Ḥunayn and Khaybar, for example.

However, as God had granted her a long life there were yet more scenes for her eyes to witness. It was destined that the baby she held from birth, whom she had watched grow to manhood, then be honoured with Prophethood, was now to end his life before her eyes too. The passing away of the Prophet ﷺ was a time of great sorrow; the loss of the only human connection to the last revelation of God on High. Barakah ؓ, like all the members of his family and the believers, was deeply saddened. She wept at the loss of the Prophet ﷺ, but also 'because now revelation has come to an end', as she told the great Companion, 'Umar ؓ.

Barakah's own son, Ayman, had also died – he was martyred at the Battle of Ḥunayn. He was a devoted Companion of the noble Prophet ﷺ and was raised by his mother to serve the needs of the growing community of believers. Her younger son, Usāmah, at the age of seventeen, was given a weighty responsibility by the noble Prophet ﷺ to lead a massive force against the Byzantines. It was the last appointment that the Prophet ﷺ made before he passed away and it was left to the wise Abū Bakr ﷺ to confirm the commission.

In the last days of her life, Barakah ﷺ held a position of honour and glowing respect within the Madinan community. She was like a beacon, whose light brightened the lives of those around her. Aging was no hindrance to this noble lady, on the contrary, her inner beauty and bravery only got stronger.

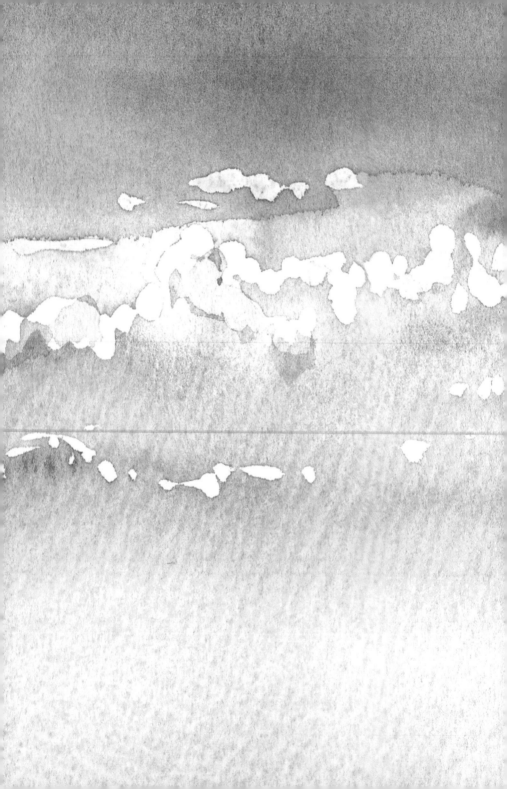

The Soul's Journey On...

The Shoreline

Every soul shall taste death, then in the end to Us shall you all be returned. (Surah al-'Ankabūt 29:57)

The Soul's Journey On...

We all share one certainty: that we will face the end of this mortal life on earth. For some souls there is a preparation period, a forewarning that their soul's journey is drawing close. For others there are no signs; a sudden swift departure, or silently slipping away without bidding farewell to the dawn. Each parting from this life is incomparable, likewise the timing of this departure/passage – infant, child, mid-life or as an elder – is unknown to us

Though each life is a journey, be it through rough waves or floating on calm quiescent waters, the soul's destination is always in view. We know this life on earth is not eternal, it will come to an end and the next life awaits us, and understanding the reality of death and the Hereafter is what brings meaning to this world. In order to navigate in the right direction, we need to know why we are here and where we are going.

Seeing things with our hearts and minds will show us in this life some aspects of the Hereafter, such as rainfall bringing the dead, dry earth back to life, or the salmon that travels thousands of miles through the oceans to return, in the end, back to their home; the place from which they began. Such is the case with our souls that journey back to their Creator, back to the home we have earned in the Hereafter.

Each of us knows of someone who has passed away. Their time in this world is finished, and there is no return. Nonetheless, we still have the silent testimony of time, our breath, we still have hearts that beat, eyelids that open and close without effort. With each blink, our eyes capture a 'photo' of this world. Then it is gone, that second has elapsed and we carry on storing worldly views countless times a day; 'passing time'. Yet we still have time to steer towards Jannah, our goal, moving in the direction of sincerity in word and deed, in the hope of earning God's pleasure.

Where are we going? What is our destination? In which direction have we set our internal compass? Journeys take us where we set out to go. As we ride the waves, which carry us through our lives, there comes a point where the sea meets the sand, and we arrive at the shoreline. As the water washes over the sand, the seamless shore is created.

So too with the end of this worldly life, and the transition into the next. The motion of moving from one to the other happens as subtly as the waves washing onto the shore – we enter the next life. Our world, our life, our pulse, our breath will depart like a retreating tide. As our soul glides to the shoreline, our life's worth leaves a trail in the waves; a legacy or a liability, the Hereafter will tell us. Until the moment of death arrives, there is hope – each dawn is an invitation of hope. There is still time to honour life and its purpose, to invest in making the destination of the Hereafter a place of eternal rest, by *al-Raḥmān*'s, the All Merciful's, decree; a place of peace.

Myriad Voices

'I look out each night at the cobalt sky and the stencil of russet branches against it. Unafraid, the trees stand tall, defiant and unwavering. Conquering stillness, just being, silently alive. While I watch the trellis of branches resting on the expansive, unending sky, the inner eye imagines their roots, unseen and entwined in the earth. The same earth that will be my next home.
Beneath the roots, or beside them, taking my place beneath the layers.
Where will my vision, that I gaze with intently, be then?
Will death eclipse all shades of darkness, all hues of light, an existence in the penumbra?
Or, at that time, will the earth and the sky cease to exist to my departed soul?
As each night passes, I am one step closer to joining the roots of that tree.
What did my soul earn today to take into that darkness?
What light did it gather to light my grave, what blessings to widen my grave, what forgiveness sought to ease my stay?'

The Soul's Journey On...

'Now that my time has arrived, no longer can I lean on my old friend of excuses. My life was ordained and has reached beyond six decades; no longer can I say,
'if only I had more time'.
Sufficient was the time to collect my provisions for the next stage of my soul's journey.
Plentiful were my opportunities to earn for the next, more permanent stage of my existence.

No more time to look back,
no more time.'

'I open with the first glint of light each morning. I have
witnessed guests arriving for decades. One by one, the empty
spaces housing their white-sheeted residents. Day in and night
out, there is a constant register of those leaving this world. An
even-handed register calling the young, the healthy, the frail,
the ill. Today another occupant arrives – relatives staring into
the dusk – for the first time some eyes widen and see reality.
Each guest thought their life on the other side of my
wrought-iron barrier was far away – life would last forever –
how wrong they were! This is their long-term home now and
I, merely the gate that separates them; dutifully opening and
closing each day.
Family members exit past me in haste, their footsteps heavy.
Tongues silenced as they swallow back emotion, hearts shaken
and souls awakened. They fear their next meeting with me;
will it be as an occupant, or as a bystander accompanying a
loved one?
Slate ink blots out the saffron tufts in the sky, signalling it's
time to close.
For the new occupants, their time here has just begun.'

'Which night will be the last; which night will be the final one that I sleep on this side of the sky, the side I know and have grown so attached to?
Will I recognize my final night on earth as the last one? Will there be some way of knowing – a sign, perhaps?
And, when I make the turn into the other side of the sky, will my lips support my soul by affirming its belief and final truth: "I bear witness that there is nothing worthy of worship except Allah, and I bear witness that Muhammad is the Messenger of Allah?"'
(*Ash-hadu an lā ilāha illā Allāh wa ash-hadu anna Muḥammadan Rasūl Allāh.*)

'Now that death is imminent, my soul is soon to be drawn out. Why did I scoff at those who lived their lives as though on the threshold of death? Why did I laugh at their distance from the luxuries and possessions of this world, which I am now leaving behind? Not a brick of my mansion am I taking with me, nor my gems or costumes of wealth or fame. How could I have derided those whose hearts understood the reality which, only *now* I realize?'

'What will be left when I am gone?
The sun and moon will still run their courses and bring day and night to all who have been given time. The trees will still bloom, and rain will fall.
Each dawn will witness the multitude of homes stirring back to life after the stillness of the night. Their lights will burn,

their water flow and steaming cups will rouse them to their
new day.
But not mine.
The birds at first light will come, eat their crumbs thrown out
to them,
But not mine.
Will the world continue the same?
Or does the world alter – its axis tilt minutely – each time
someone dies?
Does a world die with each person; their own, personal, daily
world full of patterns and habits, stops and starts?
As I leave, my world will slip away too.
All that remains in this world is any truth imparted, and good
planted; may they continue to grow and prosper long after my
passing away.'

The Eternal Sources

Once our time in this world is fulfilled, the departure from it – death – is a reality we are reminded of time and again. Allah is *al-Mubdi'*, the Originator, *al-Qabīd*, the Taker, from Whom life originates and to Whom it returns. In recognizing this comes the comfort and reality that both life and death are beyond any person's control.

Does man think that We shall not be able to put his bones back together?
In fact, We can reshape his very fingertips.
Yet man wants to deny what is ahead of him: he asks, 'So, when will this Day of Resurrection be?'
When eyes are dazzled, and the moon eclipsed, when the sun and the moon are brought together, on that Day man will say, 'Where can I escape?'
Truly, there is no refuge: they will all return to your Lord that Day.
On that Day, man will be told what he put first and what he put last.
Truly, man is a clear witness against himself, despite all the excuses he may put forward. (Surah *al-Qiyāmah* 75:3–15)

It is He Who gives life and causes death; and when He decides upon a matter, He only says to it, 'Be', and it is. (Surah *al-Mu'min* 40:68)

How can you reject and be ungrateful to Allah, seeing that you were without life and He gave you life, then He will cause you to die and will again bring you back to life; and again to Him will you return. (Surah *al-Baqarah* 2:28)

It is God Who takes away the souls [of people] at the time of death, and those that die not [He takes] during their sleep. Those on whom He has passed the decree of death, He keeps back [from returning to life] and sends the rest for a term appointed. Indeed in this are signs for those who reflect. (Surah *al-Zumar* 39:42)

Every soul shall have a taste of death, and only on the Day of Judgment shall you be paid your full recompense. Only he who is saved far from the Fire and admitted to the Garden will have attained success [in life]. For the life of this world is but goods and chattels of deception. (Surah *Āl 'Imrān* 3:185)

To every people is a term appointed. When their term is reached, not an hour can they delay it, nor [an hour] can they advance it. (Surah *al-A'rāf* 7:34)

'Let not worldly affairs be our greatest care of all that we know about.' (Tirmidhī)

Whether our stay is short or long, this life affords us the opportunity to invest in good deeds, the only possessions we take with us to the next life. From early adulthood we start making choices about where we put our time and energy and how we prioritize our responsibilities. Each person is responsible for what they take into the next life, either seeking the bounty and mercy of their Sustainer, or not.

No bearer of burdens can bear another's burden. If someone who is weighed down calls for help to bear his load, none of it will be borne for him, even by his next of kin. You can only warn those who fear their Sovereign Sustainer in the Unseen and establish ṣalāt (prayer). Whoever is purified, is purified for himself alone. Allah is your final destination. (Surah *Fāṭir* 35:18)

That Day people will proceed in companies sorted out, to be shown the deeds that they [had done]. Whoever does an atom's weight of good will see it; and whoever does an atom's weight of evil will see it. (Surah *al-Zilzāl* 99:6–8)

'The Prophet ﷺ said: "Some of the deeds and the rewards that follow a believer after death are: knowledge that he taught or published; a good child that he left behind; a Qur'an that he bequeathed to someone; a mosque that he built; a house that he built for the wayfarer; a river that he rented (to be used free); or a charity that he gave from his wealth during his good health and his life. These are the ones that follow a person after his death."' (Ibn Mājah)

'A man came to the Prophet ﷺ and said, "My mother has died! And she had to do a month's fasting – so should I fulfil this obligation on her behalf?"
"Yes," replied the Prophet ﷺ. "God's debt is the one to be repaid above all others."' (Bukhārī)

'Three things follow the bier of a dead man. Two of them come back and one is left with him: the members of his family, wealth and his good deeds. The members of his family and wealth come back and the deeds alone are left with him.' (Muslim)

The whisper of the *adhān* into the new-born's ears ushers the soul into its worldly existence. As our soul is bid

farewell from this world, the *iqāmah* is called for the *janāzah* (funeral); this is how short our time is here on this earth. This life we have cried over, fought over, rejoiced over, chased with all our being, lasts the time between the *adhān* and *iqāmah*. As we exit from this world, we pass through the honourable rites of passage to the Hereafter. The first encounter at this time is meeting the angels of death.

'Allah's Messenger ﷺ said, "Encourage those of you who are dying to recite, 'There is no god but Allah'."' (Muslim)

Why then, when death reaches one's throat and you are at that moment looking on – at that moment We are nearer him than you, though you cannot see [Us]. (Surah *al-Wāqi'ah* 56:83–85)

[The God-conscious are] those whose lives the angels take in a state of purity, saying [to them]: 'Peace be on you; enter Paradise, because of [the good] which you used to do [in the world].' (Surah *al-Naḥl* 16:32)

It is prescribed that when death approaches any of you, if he leave behind any goods that he make a bequest to parents and next of kin, according to reasonable usage; a duty from those who have taqwā [God consciousness]. (Surah *al-Baqarah* 2:180)

And they say: 'What! When we lie, hidden and lost in the earth, shall we indeed be created renewed?' Still, they deny the meeting with their Sustainer. Say: 'The angel of death has been put in charge of you and will [duly] take your souls. Then shall you all be brought back to your Sustainer.' If only you could see the guilty ones with their heads bent low before their Sustainer, [saying]:

'Our Sustainer! We have seen and we have heard. Now send us back [to the world] and we will work righteously, for we do indeed [now] believe.' (Surah *al-Sajdah* 32:10-12)

Indeed, those who say, 'Our Sustainer is Allah', and then stand firm [on the straight path], angels will descend on them [at the time of death] saying: 'Fear not and do not grieve, but receive the glad tidings of the Paradise which you were promised!
We are your protectors in this life and in the Hereafter. There you shall have all that your souls shall desire and there you shall have all that you ask for – a hospitable gift from One most Forgiving, ever Merciful!' (Surah *Fuṣṣilāt* 41:30–32)

'Umm 'Aṭiyah said, "When the daughter of the Prophet ﷺ died, he came to us and said: 'Wash her three or five times, or more than that if you deem it necessary, with water and lotus blossoms, and then finally put camphor – or anything similar. Then notify me when you have finished.'
So when we had finished what he had told us to do, we notified him, and he gave us his waist wrapper and he said: 'Clothe her in this'.'" (Bukhārī)

In the life of the world, we make our homes to suit our needs. Whether a humble room or a house, this basic need for shelter, privacy and security keeps us occupied. For some people this is a life-long pursuit; forever perfecting their dwelling. For others, there is a constant struggle to find the most basic shelter and even then, when found, it can lack security. Along with the challenge of home-making in this life, is the reality of our unseen homes in the next life. The first 'home' in the Hereafter is the grave. Whether we find ease, space and security there, is related

to how much of our life we invested in this unseen home. Unlike our earthly home, this location is not bought with wealth; the only currency is our conduct. The eternal home grows from our intentions and sincerity. What were we willing to sacrifice in the world for our residence in the Hereafter?

'The Messenger of God ﷺ said, "When the dead man is laid in his grave it speaks to him, saying, 'Woe betide you, O son of Adam! What distracted you from contemplating me? Did you not know that I am the house of trial, the house of darkness, the house of solitude and the house of worms? What distracted you from me? You used to pass me by, strutting on!' Now if he had worked well, then someone will reply to the grave on his behalf, saying, 'Do you not see that it was his practice to enjoin the good and forbid the evil?' And the grave replies, 'Then for him shall I turn to verdure [a condition of freshness or healthy growth], and his body shall become radiant, and his spirit shall soar up to God – Exalted is He!'." (Tirmidhī)

'The Messenger of God ﷺ once declared: "The dead man sits up and hears the footsteps of those that are present at his funeral, but none addresses him save his tomb, which says, 'Woe betide you, O son of Adam! Did you not fear me and my narrowness, and my corruption, terror and worms? What have you prepared for me?'." (Ibn al-Mubārak)

Beyond the perception of our faculties, we are promised the experience of the Final Hour and we will witness the scenes from the Day of Rising. On that Day, time, our lives and the earth as we know it will take on a new dimension.

*They ask you about the [Final] Hour, when will be its appointed
time? Say: 'The knowledge thereof is with my Sustainer [alone]:
None but He can reveal when it will occur. Heavy will be its
burden on the heavens and the earth. Only, all of a sudden will
it come to you.' They ask you, as if you were eager in search of it.
Say: 'The knowledge thereof is with Allah [alone], but most people
know not.'* (Surah *al-A'rāf* 7:187)

When the sky is cleft asunder,
when the stars are scattered,
when the oceans burst forth,
and when graves are turned upside down –
[Then] shall each soul know what it has sent forward and [what
it has] kept back.
O man! What has deceived you from Your Sustainer, the Most
Generous? (Surah *al-Infiṭār* 82:1–6)

Say: 'Do you think that if the punishment of Allah were to come
upon you, or the Hour were to come upon you, would you then
call upon other than Allah [for help], if you are truthful?'
(Surah *al-An'ām* 6:40)

To Him is referred the Knowledge of the Hour [of Judgment. He
knows all]: No fruit comes out of its sheath, nor does a female
conceive [within her womb] nor bring forth [young], but by His
knowledge. That Day [Allah] will call out to them: 'Where are
the partners [you attributed] to Me?' They will say, 'We do assure
You not one of us can bear witness!' (Surah *Fuṣṣilāt* 41:47)

And on the day when He will gather them together, [it will be] as
if they had tarried but an hour of a day to get to know each other.
Assuredly, those who denied meeting with Allah and refused to
receive true guidance will be lost. (Surah *Yūnus* 10:45)

Then when the Trumpet is blown, there will be no more relationships between them that Day, nor will one ask after another! Then those whose balance [of good deeds] is heavy, they will attain salvation.

But those whose balance is light, they will have lost their souls; in Hell will they abide. (Surah *al-Mu'minūn* 23:101–103)

'A man asked the Prophet ﷺ, "When will the Hour be established, O Messenger of Allah?" The Prophet ﷺ said, "What have you prepared for it?" The man said, "I haven't prepared for it much of prayers or fasting or alms, but I love Allah and His Messenger.' The Prophet ﷺ said, "You will be with those whom you love."' (Bukhārī)

They ask you [Prophet] about the Hour, saying 'When will it arrive?' But how can you tell them that? Its time is known only to your Lord, you are only sent to warn those who fear it. On the Day they see it, it will seem they lingered [in this life] at most one evening, or one morning. (Surah *al-Nāzi'āt* 79:42–46)

The soul is destined to return to *al-Ṣamad*, the Eternal, from whence it came. Our soul's home is Jannah, and it yearns for this return. As much as we know that our lives here are not the 'end' – that they are a means to an end in the Hereafter – we forget to invest in this reality. To forget is human, as the roots of the word '*insān*' suggests. We still have time to focus on what we sow here and what we will reap there.

And to every human being, We have fastened his destiny to his neck. On the Day of Resurrection, We shall bring forth for him a

record which he will find wide open, [saying]:
'Read your record! This Day, your own self is enough as a reckoner
against you.' (Surah Banī Isrā'īl 17:13–14)

Nay, the truth is that you love this fleeting life and ignore the
Hereafter.
Some faces on that Day will beam [with brightness and beauty],
looking towards their Sustainer; and some faces that Day will be
sad and dismal, in the thought that some back-breaking calamity
is about to be inflicted on them.
Yea, when [the soul] reaches to the collar-bone [in its exit] there
will be a cry: 'Is there any magician here [to restore him]?
And he will conclude that it is [the Time] of Parting.
(Surah *al-Qiyāmah* 75:20-28)

'As to those who believe and do righteous deeds, they will have for
their entertainment the Gardens of Paradise, Wherein they shall
dwell forever, with no desire to be removed from there.'
(Surah *al-Kahf* 18:107–108)

If any do deeds of righteousness – be they male or female – and
have faith, they will enter Heaven and not the least injustice will
be done to them. (Surah al-Nisā' 4:124)

Nay, whoever submits his whole self to Allah and is a doer of good,
he will get his reward with his Lord. On such shall be no fear, nor
shall they grieve. (Surah al-Baqarah 2:112)

And obey Allah and the Messenger; that ye may obtain mercy.
Be quick in the race for forgiveness from your Lord, and for a
Garden whose width is that [of the whole] of the heavens and of
the earth, prepared for the righteous.

*Those who spend [freely], whether in prosperity or in adversity;
who restrain anger and pardon [all] men, Allah loves those who
do good.* (Surah Āl 'Imrān 3:132–134)

*And those who, having done something to be ashamed of, or who
have wronged their own souls, instantly remember Allah and
ask for forgiveness for their sins – and who can forgive sins
except Allah? – and do not knowingly persist in [the wrong]
they have done.
For such the reward is forgiveness from their Lord, and Gardens
with rivers flowing underneath, an eternal dwelling. How
excellent a recompense for those who work [and strive]!*
(Surah Āl 'Imrān 3:135–136)

*How excellent is the abode of the God-fearing: Gardens of Eternity
which they will enter, beneath them flowing [pleasant] rivers.
They will have therein all that they wish; thus Allah rewards the
righteous.* (Surah al-Naḥl 16:30-31)

'The Messenger of Allah ﷺ said: "Allah will say on the Day of
Resurrection: 'Where are those who love one another through
My glory? Today I shall give them shade in My shade, it being
a day when there is no shade but My shade'.'" (Bukhārī)

'The Messenger of Allah ﷺ said: "Allah, Glorified and Exalted
is He, said: 'I have prepared for My righteous servants what
no eye has seen and no ear has heard, not has it occurred to
a human heart. Thus recite if you wish "*And no soul knows
what joy for them [the inhabitants of Paradise] has been kept
hidden*"'." (32:17)

'The Messenger of Allah ﷺ said: "Allah, Glorified and Exalted is He, says: 'My faithful servant's reward from Me, if I have taken to Me his best friend from among the inhabitants of the world and he has then borne it patiently for My sake, shall be nothing less than Paradise'."' (Bukhārī – *Ḥadīth Qudsī*)

'The Messenger of Allah ﷺ said, Exalted is He, said: "If My servant likes to meet Me, I like to meet him; and if he dislikes to meet Me, I dislike to meet him."
The Prophet ﷺ explained the above hadith in the following way: "He who likes to meet Allah, Allah likes to meet him; and he who dislikes to meet Allah, Allah dislikes to meet him."
'Ā'ishah ﷺ said: "O Prophet of Allah, is it because of the dislike of death, for all of us dislike death?" The Prophet ﷺ said: "It is not so, but rather it is that when the believer is given news of Allah's mercy, His approval and His Paradise, he likes to meet Allah and Allah likes to meet him; but when the unbeliever is given news of Allah's punishment and His displeasure, he dislikes to meet Allah and Allah dislikes to meet him."' (*Ḥadīth Qudsī*)

'It was said to the Prophet ﷺ; "A man may love some people but he cannot catch up with their good deeds?" The Prophet ﷺ said, "Everyone will be with those whom he loves."' (Bukhārī)

'The Prophet ﷺ said: "(In order to enter Paradise) you should worship Allah and do not ascribe any partners to Him, offer Prayer perfectly, pay the Zakat and keep good relations with your kith and kin."' (Bukhārī)

'A Bedouin came to the Prophet ﷺ and said, "Tell me of such a deed as will make me enter Paradise, if I do it." The Prophet ﷺ said, "Worship God, and worship none along with Him, offer the (five) prescribed compulsory prayers perfectly, pay the compulsory Zakat, and fast the month of Ramadan." The Bedouin said, "By Him, in Whose hands my life is, I will not do more than this." When he (the Bedouin) left, the Prophet ﷺ said, "Whoever likes to see a man of Paradise, then he may look at this man."' (Bukhārī)

''Abdullāh ibn Mas'ūd ﷺ narrated. The Prophet ﷺ said: "Should I inform you about those whom the Hellfire is forbidden to burn or who is forbidden for the Fire? The fire is forbidden to touch every person who is gentle, soft-spoken, and easy to deal with."' (Tirmidhī)

*Du ʿāʾ*s for the Soul's Journey

These *duʿāʾ*s take our hearts to an unfamiliar place, the unseen Hereafter, and at the same time they encompass the painfully familiar subject of death – that tangible reality around us. The essence of these *duʿāʾ*s is to prioritize our eternal soul. We are reminded repeatedly in the sacred sources that life and death were created *'to test you and reveal which of you does best'* (Surah *al-Mulk* 67:2) and in these supplications we ask for our souls to have the best outcome; eternal peace through the pleasure of *al-Ghaffār* – the Ever Forgiving, *al-Ḥakam*, the Judge. At the same time, these *duʿāʾ*s connect us to our lineage, asking for forgiveness on behalf of our loved ones who have passed before us and for those whose souls depart in front of us. Above all, these supplications reinstate the reality of our physical life ending and our *rūḥ* continuing, a reality that fades all too easily into the background of daily life. Remembrance of death softens our hearts and clears the mind, connecting us back to the origin of our souls.

'Allah's Messenger ﷺ said,
"Whenever you go to your bed (to sleep) say:
'O Allah! I have surrendered myself over to you, and
have turned my face towards You,
and leave all my affairs to You,
and depend on You,
and put my trust in You expecting Your reward and fearing Your punishment.
There is neither fleeing from You nor refuge but with You.
I believe in the Book (Qur'an) which You have revealed and in Your Prophet (Muhammad) whom You have sent.' If you then die on that night, then you will die as a Muslim, and if you

wake alive in the morning then you will receive the reward.'"
(Bukhārī)

'Jubayr ibn Nufayr says: "I heard it from 'Awf ibn Mālik that
the Prophet's prayer on a dead body… 'O Allah! Forgive
him, have mercy upon him, give him peace and absolve him.
Receive him with honour and make his grave spacious; wash
him with water, snow and hail.
Cleanse him from faults as You would cleanse a white garment
from impurity. Requite him with an abode more excellent
than his abode, with a family better than his family, and with
a spouse better than his spouse.
Admit him to Paradise, and protect him from the torment of
the grave and the torment of the Fire'.'" (Muslim)

'At the time of closing the eyes of the deceased:

"O Allah! Forgive… and raise his rank among the rightly-
guided, and be a successor to whom he has left behind, and
forgive us and him O Sovereign Sustainer of all creation.
Make spacious his grave and illuminate it for him.'" (Muslim)

'O Allah! Forgive our living and our dead, those present and
those absent, our young and our old, our males and our
females. O Allah, whom amongst us You keep alive, then let
such a life be upon Islam, and who amongst us You take unto
Yourself, then let such a death be upon faith. O Allah, do not
deprive us of his reward, and do not let us stray after him.'
(Ibn Majāh)

'O Allah! So and so is under Your care and protection so
protect him from the trial of the grave and the torment of the

Fire. Indeed, You are the faithful and truthful. Forgive and have mercy upon him, surely You are the Oft-Forgiving, the Most Merciful.' (Abū Dāwūd)

'O Allah! I seek refuge with you from the punishment in the grave and from the punishment in the Hell-fire and from the *fitnah* (trials and tribulations) of life and death; and the *fitnah* of *al-Masīḥ al-Dajjāl*.' (Bukhārī)

'O Allah! By Your knowledge of the unseen and Your power to create, grant me life as long as You know that life is best for me, and take me when You know that death is best for me. O Allah! I ask You for fear of You both within my secret heart and openly. I ask You for the word of truth in pleasure and anger. I ask You for moderation both in poverty and riches. I ask You for felicity which does not pass away. I ask You for comfort which is not cut off. I ask You for satisfaction with what is decreed. I ask You for a pleasant life after death. I ask You for the pleasure of looking at Your countenance, and longing to meet You in a state in which distress does not cause harm or testing leads astray.
O Allah! Beautify us with the adornment of faith, and make us among those who are rightly-guided.' (Nasā'ī)

'Abū Umāmah said: "The Prophet ﷺ used to make many *duʿā*'s. Shall I teach you a *duʿā*' which sums up the rest? Say: 'O Allah, I ask You the best of what Your Prophet Muhammad asked you for, and I seek refuge with You from the worst of what Your Prophet Muhammad sought your protection against.

You are the One we can turn to for help and support, and You are the One Who can guide us to our destination. There is neither strength nor power except with the help of Allah'." (*Kanz al-'Ummāl*)

When Righteous Souls Depart

Nay! I call to witness the sunset's fleeting afterglow,
And the night and what it unfolds,
And by the moon, as it grows to fullness, that
you are bound to move onwards from stage to stage.
(Surah *al-Inshiqāq* 84:16–19)

In previous chapters, we have taken a glimpse of the lives of virtuous and noble women. Collectively, their lives span centuries. Some responded to the call to believe in One God; others were mothers and wives of the Prophets. Though their historical settings differed, they were united in their belief and ultimately in their righteous death. The accounts of their lives have become stories, passed from generation to generation, and the contents of many a book. Their time on earth has passed, yet their virtues remain alive and available for us to take heed of.

All of the righteous women, different in worldly status and experiences, held to one handhold: belief in the One True God. The rope they clung to could not be severed by anything. No amount of contemporary culture, social pressure, emotional or physical threats could sever the rope of 'Islam' they gripped so firmly. Neither did the common worry of social pressures and people's opinions deter them in their cause of establishing the Truth and living moral lives.

Nor were the lives of these noble souls free of troubles. An array of problems beset them, ranging from family deaths, widowhood, poverty and homelessness; even slander and wrong accusations were levelled at some of them. Furthermore, they were not exempt from the struggles within themselves either: fear, uncertainty, sadness and pain are a few of their inner states that challenged them. With their heightened awareness, they would regularly evaluate the condition of their hearts. Much of what they passed through has many parallels in today's world.

Death came to them at different ages and in different ways. The death of Asmā' ✿, the daughter of the first righteous Caliph Abū Bakr ✿, illustrates the state of mind of an elderly lady, who passed away at the age of one hundred years. When her life was ending, her spirit remained as strong and courageous as it was in her youth. Age took its toll upon her physically, as she was blind and frail, yet when her son 'Abdullāh ibn Zubayr ✿ came to seek her advice before embarking on a treacherous battle, she gave him hope and courage to stand his ground in the struggle for truth. She knew her son and his army had little prospect of victory, and she supplicated for him before he went to meet his destiny:

> O Allah, have mercy on his staying up for long hours and his loud crying in the darkness of the night while people slept…
> O Allah, have mercy on his hunger and his thirst on his journeys from Madinah and Makkah while he fasted.
> O Allah, bless his righteousness to his mother and his father.
> O Allah, I commend him to Your cause and I am pleased with whatever You decree for him. And grant me for his sake the reward of those who are patient and who persevere.

'Abdullāh's soul passed away the same day. Asmā' 🌸, who was granted a long life, died only ten days later. May her soul be blessed.

In contrast, the death of the Prophet Muhammad's daughter, Fāṭimah 🌸 occurred when she was in the prime of her youth. At the age of twenty-nine, in the same year of her father's death, it was destined that her worldly life would come to a close. It is reported that Fāṭimah 🌸 rarely smiled after her father's death; her distance from his noble person caused her much sadness.

The day her soul was to leave this world, she was more cheerful than usual. The virtuous daughter of the Prophet 🌸 prepared herself as one would for a special day, and then called for her husband – the noble Companion and fourth Caliph, 'Alī 🌸. 'Today', she said, 'I have a meeting with the Messenger of Allah 🌸.' This, of course, brought tears to her husband's eyes. She consoled him, reminding him of the care and attention their sons Ḥasan and Ḥusayn would need. Looking up into the vastness of the heavenly bodies, she closed her eyes and her soul returned to Allah, the Sovereign Sustainer of all humankind.

Both believers' souls were taken back to their Creator at different ages, yet there was no anxiety about death, or anguish about leaving this world. The destination of the Hereafter was always the focus of their lives. Their objective of success in the next life shaped their conduct, in turn influencing the societies in which they lived and leaving a legacy of their principles and conduct to enrich the world. They exemplified the pithy but powerful piece of advice of 'Umar ibn al-Khaṭṭāb 🌸:

'Work for this world as if you would live forever, and prepare
for the next as though you will die tomorrow.'

> Verily, that which is with
> Allah is best for you,
> if you but knew: all that
> you have is bound to end,
> whereas all that is with
> Allah is everlasting.
> (Surah *al-Naḥl* 16:95–96)

Glossary of Arabic Words

Ākhirah: The next world, what is on the other side of death, the Hereafter. It is a dimension of existence beyond this worldly mortal life and is described in the Qur'an as 'better and more lasting'.

Allāhu Akbar: God is Most Great.

Amānah: Trust, responsibility.

Angels: A species of God's creatures always obedient to His will.

'Aqd al-Nikāḥ: A written marriage contract signed by the bride and the groom and witnessed by two adult and sane witnesses.

Āyah (**pl.** *āyāt*): A sign; a miracle; a message, a verse of the Qur'an. *Āyāt* refers to the signs one sees in nature, in ourselves, and in all forms of creation.

Birr: Righteousness, virtue; fidelity in discharging obligations.

Dhikr: Remembrance or reminding oneself of God through various devotional practices. In general terms, all worship is *dhikr*. Specifically, it has come to mean remembering God by reciting the *Asmā' al-Ḥusnā*, His beautiful names and attributes, repeating virtuous expressions such as '*Al-Ḥamdulillāh*' (all praise and gratitude is due to Allah), '*SubḥānAllāh*' (glorified and exalted is He), and '*Allāhu Akbar*' (Allah is Most Great).

Du'ā': Supplication to Allah. This can be in one's own words, as well as the numerous supplications cited in the Qur'an and taught by Prophet Muhammad ﷺ.

***Hadith* (plural, *aḥādīth*):** A saying or tradition of the Prophet Muhammad ﷺ. The hadith form an essential part of the Prophet's Sunnah, or life example, which includes what he said, what he did and what he approved.

Ḥadīth Qudsī: (Literally, 'Sacred Hadith'.) The meaning of such hadith was revealed to the Prophet ﷺ by God but he expressed them in his own words, unlike the Qur'an which is the word of Almighty God and the Prophet ﷺ conveyed it exactly as it was revealed to him.

Ḥayā': Modesty, shyness, sense of propriety, decency. *Ḥayā'* is part of *īmān*. A person who loses *ḥayā'*, self-destructs.

Īmān: Belief, faith, specifically intelligent faith in God. Belief consists of believing in God, His angels, His revealed books, His Messengers and the Hereafter, and that everything is by the decree of God

Jannah: (Literally, garden.) Paradise or Heaven, the abode of the righteous and the virtuous in the next life.

Jihad: (Literally, striving.) Any striving or endeavour in the way of God, whether to promote good or eradicate evil. It may take the form of private effort for self-rectification and development or social action. It may involve monetary expenditure or physical struggle.

Mujāhid: One engaged in jihad.

Nafs (**pl.** *nufūs, anfus*): Used in the Qur'an in various contexts to mean: a living entity; a being; a person; an individual; a life; nature; self; soul.

In the Qur'an there are three categories of *nafs*, or self, which are mentioned:

    i. The contented self (Arabic: *al-nafs al-muṭma'innah*). This refers to the person who remains stable and unshaken in his or her devotion to God in all circumstances, whether in ease or hardship, neither becoming proud and smug in times of success nor impatient and fretful in times of difficulty. (See, Surah *al-Fajr* 89: 27–30)

    ii. The censorious self (Arabic: *al-nafs al-lawwāmah*). The part of human nature which represents the urge to goodness, and censures a person before or after committing an evil act. In other words, it is the conscience of the human being. It is opposed to 'the bidding or tempting self'. (See, Surah *al-Qiyāmah* 75: 2)

    iii. The bidding or tempting self (Arabic: *al-nafs al-ammārah bi-s sū*). The part of the human being that tempts him or her to commit evil. (See, Surah *Yūsuf* 12: 53)

Nikāḥ: Marriage. The Prophet Muhammad ﷺ said: 'Marriage (*al-Nikāḥ*) is part of my Sunnah. Whoever consciously departs from my Sunnah is not of me.'

Qur'an: (Literally, the Recitation.) The last revealed scripture from God to humankind. It was revealed to the Prophet Muhammad ﷺ through the angel Jibrīl over a period of twenty-three years beginning in the year 610 CE. It remains intact and preserved exactly as it was revealed.

Rūḥ (**pl. arwāḥ**): Breath of life; spirit; soul. That part of a person's being which lives on beyond physical death. Also used in the Qur'an for the Angel Jibrīl

Ṣalāh: An Arabic word to mean a spiritual relationship and communication between the creature and his or her Creator. *Ṣalāh* is one of the five pillars of Islam and is performed in the manner as demonstrated by the Prophet Muhammad ﷺ. The obligatory *ṣalāh* is performed five times a day: between dawn (Fajr) and sunrise, early afternoon (Ẓuhr), late afternoon ('Aṣr), just after sunset (Maghrib) and at night ('Ishā'). *Ṣalāh* is performed with mental concentration, verbal communication, vocal recitation, and physical movement to attain spiritual uplift, peace and harmony.

Sujūd: Prostration to Allah as part of *ṣalāh* in which the worshipper praises and glorifies his Creator, the Most Sublime.

Surah: A chapter of the Qur'an, composed of *āyāt* or verses. There are one hundred and fourteen surahs in the Qur'an. Each surah has a name linked to a main theme within it.

Tahajjud: Prayer. Voluntary *ṣalāh* performed after sleeping after the 'Ishā' Prayer and before dawn breaks. A blessed time in which believers are encouraged to wake up and reap the benefits of drawing close to God, Most High.

223

Taqwā: The awareness of God, and the love and fear that a person feels for Him. A person with *taqwā* desires to be in the good pleasures of Allah and to stay away from those things that would displease Him. He is careful not to go beyond the bounds and limits set by Allah. Translated variously as 'self-restraint', 'piety', 'God-consciousness' and 'righteousness'.

Zakat: The compulsory 'purifying' tax on wealth which is one of the five pillars of Islam. The word zakat is derived from the word meaning purification, growth and sweetening.

Further Reading

General

Badawi, J. A., *Selected Prayers* (London: Ta-Ha Publishers, 2006).

Eaton, G., *Islam and the Destiny of Man* (Cambridge: The Islamic Texts Society, 1994).

Hamid, A. W., *Islam the Natural Way* (London: Muslim Education and Literary Services, 2004).

Hamid, A. W., *Companions of the Prophet, volumes 1 and 2* (London: Muslim Education and Literary Services, 2014).

Islam, Y., *Prayers of the Last Prophet*, CD, MC and book (London: Mountain of Light Productions, 1998).

al-Mubarakpuri, S., *The Sealed Nectar: Ar-Raheeq Al-Makhtum* (Riyadh: Dar-us-Salam Publications, 2010).

Murad, K., *Way to the Qur'an* (Leicester: The Islamic Foundation, 1985).

Sarwar, G., *Islam: Beliefs and Teachings* (London: Muslim Educational Trust, 2006).

Women and Motherhood

Badawi, J. A., *Gender Equity in Islam: Basic Principles* (Indianapolis: American Trust Publications, 2005).

Bari, M. A., *Building Muslim Families* (London: Ta-Ha Publishers, 2002).

Bari, M. A., *The Greatest Gift: A Guide to Parenting From an Islamic Perspective* (London: Ta-Ha Publishers, 2003).

Bewley, A., *Islam: The Empowering of Women* (London: Ta-Ha Publishers, 1999).

Khattab, H., *The Bent Rib: A Journey Through Women's Issues in Islam* (London: Ta-Ha Publishers, 1997).

Schleifer, A., *Motherhood in Islam* (Cambridge: Islamic Texts Society, 1986).

Tarazi, N., *The Child in Islam* (Indianapolis: American Trust Publications, 1995).

Contemplation and Spiritual Development

Badri, M., *Contemplation: An Islamic Psychospiritual Study* (Herndon VA: The International Institute of Islamic Thought, 2000).

al-Bayhaki, A. B., and T. J. Winter (trans.), *The Seventy-Seven Branches of Faith* (London: Quillam Press, 1990).

al-Ghazali, A. H., and M. Holland (trans.), *Inner Dimensions of Islamic Worship: From Iḥiyā' 'Ulūm Ad-Dīn* (Leicester: The Islamic Foundation, Leicester, 1992).

Hamid, A. W., *Burnishing the Heart* (London: Muslim Education and Literary Services, 2008).

Murad, K., *In the Early Hours: Reflections on Spiritual & Self Development* (Leicester: The Islamic Foundation, 1999).

Ibn Qayyim al-Jawziyyah, and al-Khattab, N. (trans.), *Patience and Gratitude* (London: Ta-Ha Publishers, 1997).

Islam and Nature

Abdel Haleem, H. (ed.), *Islam and the Environment* (London: Ta-Ha Publishers, 2008).

Notes

Notes

And ask forgiveness from your Lord
and turn to Him in repentance.
Verily, my Lord is Most Merciful, Most Loving.

(Surah *Hūd* 11: 90)